OPPOSING VIEWPOINTS® SERIES

Violent Video Games and Society

Other Books of Related Interest

Opposing Viewpoints Series

Gun Violence
Media Violence
Video Games
Virtual Reality

At Issue Series

Does the Internet Increase Anxiety?
Does the Internet Increase Crime?
Is Media Violence a Problem?
Violent Video Games

Current Controversies Series

Cybercrime
Guns and Violence
Media Ethics
Violence in the Media

> "Congress shall make no law ... abridging the freedom of speech, or of the press."
>
> *First Amendment to the US Constitution*

The basic foundation of our democracy is the First Amendment guarantee of freedom of expression. The Opposing Viewpoints series is dedicated to the concept of this basic freedom and the idea that it is more important to practice it than to enshrine it.

OPPOSING
VIEWPOINTS®
SERIES

Violent Video Games and Society

Gloria G. Adams, Book Editor

GREENHAVEN
PUBLISHING

Published in 2018 by Greenhaven Publishing, LLC
353 3rd Avenue, Suite 255, New York, NY 10010

Articles in Greenhaven Publishing anthologies are often edited for length to meet page
requirements. In addition, original titles of these works are changed to clearly present
the main thesis and to explicitly indicate the author's opinion. Every effort is made to
ensure that Greenhaven Publishing accurately reflects the original intent of the authors.
Every effort has been made to trace the owners of the copyrighted material.

Cover image: David J. Green - Lifestyle/Alamy Stock Photo

Library of Congress Cataloging-in-Publication Data

Names: Adams, Gloria G.
Title: Violent video games and society / Gloria G. Adams [editor].
Description: First edition. | New York : Greenhaven Publishing, 2018. | Series:
  Opposing Viewpoints | Includes bibliographical references and index.
Identifiers: LCCN 2017004977| ISBN 9781534500556 (pbk.) | ISBN
  9781534500723 (library bound)
Subjects: LCSH: Violence in video games. | Video games--Social aspects.
Classification: LCC GV1469.34 .V56 2018 | DDC 794.8--dc23
LC record available at https://lccn.loc.gov/2017004977

Manufactured in the United States of America

Website: http://greenhavenpublishing.com

Contents

Chapter 1: Can Playing Violent Video Games Alter our Behavior?

Chapter 2: What Is the Effect of Violent Video Games on Health and Development?

Chapter 3: Can Violent Video Games Lead to Extreme or Criminal Behavior?

Chapter 4: Should the Government Regulate Violent Video Games?

The Importance of Opposing Viewpoints

Perhaps every generation experiences a period in time in which the populace seems especially polarized, starkly divided on the important issues of the day and gravitating toward the far ends of the political spectrum and away from a consensus-facilitating middle ground. The world that today's students are growing up in and that they will soon enter into as active and engaged citizens is deeply fragmented in just this way. Issues relating to terrorism, immigration, women's rights, minority rights, race relations, health care, taxation, wealth and poverty, the environment, policing, military intervention, the proper role of government—in some ways, perennial issues that are freshly and uniquely urgent and vital with each new generation—are currently roiling the world.

If we are to foster a knowledgeable, responsible, active, and engaged citizenry among today's youth, we must provide them with the intellectual, interpretive, and critical-thinking tools and experience necessary to make sense of the world around them and of the all-important debates and arguments that inform it. After all, the outcome of these debates will in large measure determine the future course, prospects, and outcomes of the world and its peoples, particularly its youth. If they are to become successful members of society and productive and informed citizens, students need to learn how to evaluate the strengths and weaknesses of someone else's arguments, how to sift fact from opinion and fallacy, and how to test the relative merits and validity of their own opinions against the known facts and the best possible available information. The landmark series Opposing Viewpoints has been providing students with just such critical-thinking skills and exposure to the debates surrounding society's most urgent contemporary issues for many years, and it continues to serve this essential role with undiminished commitment, care, and rigor.

The key to the series's success in achieving its goal of sharpening students' critical-thinking and analytic skills resides in its title—

Opposing Viewpoints. In every intriguing, compelling, and engaging volume of this series, readers are presented with the widest possible spectrum of distinct viewpoints, expert opinions, and informed argumentation and commentary, supplied by some of today's leading academics, thinkers, analysts, politicians, policy makers, economists, activists, change agents, and advocates. Every opinion and argument anthologized here is presented objectively and accorded respect. There is no editorializing in any introductory text or in the arrangement and order of the pieces. No piece is included as a "straw man," an easy ideological target for cheap point-scoring. As wide and inclusive a range of viewpoints as possible is offered, with no privileging of one particular political ideology or cultural perspective over another. It is left to each individual reader to evaluate the relative merits of each argument— as he or she sees it, and with the use of ever-growing critical-thinking skills—and grapple with his or her own assumptions, beliefs, and perspectives to determine how convincing or successful any given argument is and how the reader's own stance on the issue may be modified or altered in response to it.

This process is facilitated and supported by volume, chapter, and selection introductions that provide readers with the essential context they need to begin engaging with the spotlighted issues, with the debates surrounding them, and with their own perhaps shifting or nascent opinions on them. In addition, guided reading and discussion questions encourage readers to determine the authors' point of view and purpose, interrogate and analyze the various arguments and their rhetoric and structure, evaluate the arguments' strengths and weaknesses, test their claims against available facts and evidence, judge the validity of the reasoning, and bring into clearer, sharper focus the reader's own beliefs and conclusions and how they may differ from or align with those in the collection or those of their classmates.

Research has shown that reading comprehension skills improve dramatically when students are provided with compelling, intriguing, and relevant "discussable" texts. The subject matter of these collections could not be more compelling, intriguing, or urgently relevant to today's students and the world they are poised to inherit. The anthologized articles and the reading and discussion questions that are included with them also provide the basis for stimulating, lively, and passionate classroom debates. Students who are compelled to anticipate objections to their own argument and identify the flaws in those of an opponent read more carefully, think more critically, and steep themselves in relevant context, facts, and information more thoroughly. In short, using discussable text of the kind provided by every single volume in the Opposing Viewpoints series encourages close reading, facilitates reading comprehension, fosters research, strengthens critical thinking, and greatly enlivens and energizes classroom discussion and participation. The entire learning process is deepened, extended, and strengthened.

For all of these reasons, Opposing Viewpoints continues to be exactly the right resource at exactly the right time—when we most need to provide readers with the critical-thinking tools and skills that will not only serve them well in school but also in their careers and their daily lives as decision-making family members, community members, and citizens. This series encourages respectful engagement with and analysis of opposing viewpoints and fosters a resulting increase in the strength and rigor of one's own opinions and stances. As such, it helps make readers "future ready," and that readiness will pay rich dividends for the readers themselves, for the citizenry, for our society, and for the world at large.

Introduction

> *"Every new medium has, within a short time of its introduction, been condemned as a threat to young people. Pulp novels would destroy their morals, TV would wreck their eyesight, video games would make them violent."*
>
> —Hanna Rosin, "The Touch Screen Generation," The Atlantic, *April 2013.*

The controversy over violence in entertainment media has been raging since cowboys, cops, and cartoon characters first strapped on their guns for an audience. From early comic books to TV to video games, the controversy continues: does the violence in our media have harmful effects or not?

The debate took an unexpected twist with the advent of interactive video games; no longer were we merely watching violence in the movies and on television, we were now participating in it through hand-held controllers. We could actually become a character in the game, with decision-making abilities to determine the outcome.

The controversy has heated up as games have become more violent and graphics more realistic. Parents, religious leaders, child advocates and politicians have called for bans on the games, supported scientific research studies to prove that playing violent games results in violent behavior and demanded some form of regulation. In the United States, the Entertainment Software

Ratings Board (ESRB) responded with an age-driven rating system for video game content.

Yet trying to ban the games proved unconstitutional. The ratings system, with no bite behind it, is basically just a guideline for parents and retailers, and the studies are contradictory or inconclusive. So what exactly is the impact of violent video games on our society?

Clearly, there has been an economic impact. Global gaming revenues are predicted to reach more than $105 billion in 2017. Consumers spent more than $23.5 billion on the gaming industry in 2015 and 155 million Americans play video games. But the other issues are less black and white.

A law banning violent video games was enacted by the state of California in 2005 with fines levied at non-compliant retailers. It was subsequently overturned by the Supreme Court not only because it violated First Amendment rights, but also because the judges didn't feel that there was enough evidence that violent games caused aggressive behavior to warrant passing such a ban. Many think the violent games should still be banned. Some believe the ratings by the ESRB are sufficient; others want more stringent regulations.

But what about the studies? Were the studies conducted objectively? By whom were they funded? Were other factors, such as psychological makeup of the participants, family and school situations, or mental health and medical conditions taken into consideration in all cases? Were the outcomes influenced by the agenda of those conducting the research? Why were the findings consistently contradictory?

Some studies indicated that children who played violent video games were more aggressive immediately afterward, but it was short-lived. Others blamed the aggression on frustration from not winning, and found the same level of aggression whether the game was violent or not.

Similarly, loss of empathy, dealing with stress and desensitization to violence in real life have been researched, as well as the issues of influence by the games on mass shootings, bullying and cyberbullying. All have found some connection to violent video games, but the variations are as numerous as the personalities, histories, mental health, and experiences of the people who play the games.

Only two conclusions by experts and layman alike keep surfacing in the literature surrounding violent video games. One, the effects of playing video games on people cannot be generalized because every single person brings a different pre-disposition with him or her. Two, parents should be more involved in monitoring the video games their children are playing.

In *Opposing Viewpoints: Violent Video Games and Society*, the authors examine a variety of issues related to the controversies in chapters titled "Can Playing Violent Video Games Alter our Behavior?" "What Is the Effect of Violent Video Games on Health and Development" "Can Violent Video Games Lead to Extreme or Criminal Behavior?" and "Should the Government Regulate Violent Video Games?" The divergent viewpoints will allow you to come to your own conclusions.

CHAPTER 1

Can Playing Violent Video Games Alter Our Behavior?

Chapter Preface

Make a list of aggressive behaviors in young people and chances are they have been scrutinized, researched, studied, and studied again to determine whether or not their cause can be traced back to playing violent video games. Indeed, the list of studies is as long as the list of aggressive behaviors.

Connecting violence in gaming and aggressive behavior in young people seems intuitive, yet many of the studies insist that there is no connection at all.

Those who believe that the studies prove a connection point out that the difference in playing video games and watching television is that TV viewers are merely spectators to violence while gamers are active participants, making decisions such as whether or not to kill, torture, assault, or maim. In addition, violent games reward violent behavior within the game. The question is, does this translate into violent behavior in real life? The proponents believe it does and that gamers are in denial for several reasons, both psychological and because of influence from the media and the entertainment industry.

On the other side, studies offer proof, according to the researchers, that the causes of aggression lie in our genes, that we all have aggressive tendencies and that blaming aggressive behaviors solely on violent content in video games ignores many of the other factors that contribute to aggression. One study determined that it was the frustration of losing a game, whether violent or not, or failing to reach a goal that led to aggressive behavior. Many studies see playing violent games as a possible risk factor, one of many, but not an actual cause. Others don't take into consideration pre-existing factors, such as dysfunctional family situations, abuse, problems at school, or mental health issues.

Longevity of aggression is another unresolved question. Most studies report aggression immediately following game-playing, but either found that the behavior is minimal, short-lived or don't test for longevity at all.

Politics may also play a role: are politicians looking to violent video games for a scapegoat on which to blame violent behavior in order to divert attention from guns as a cause because of pressure from NRA lobbyists?

No matter how many studies have been done, one thing seems clear: the answer is still not clear.

In the following chapter, the authors argue their cases both for and against violent video games as a cause of aggression and whether or not they have any effect on our behavior.

> "*Although the scientific evidence clearly shows that violent video games have harmful effects, many people still deny these effects, especially violent game players.*"

Violent Video Games Have Harmful Effects

Brad J. Bushman

In the following viewpoint, Brad Bushman contends that playing violent video games is more harmful than watching violent television programs or movies. Some people feel that violent games can be beneficial, but he believes that the majority of studies support the opposite viewpoint: that they cause aggressive behavior. Bushman argues that people are in denial about the links for several reasons, and are influenced by news reports of the entertainment industry's stance that their games have no harmful effects. Bushman, Ph.D., is Professor of Communication and Psychology, The Ohio State University and Professor of Communication Science, VU University, Amsterdam, the Netherlands.

"The effects of violent video games. Do they affect our behavior?" by Brad J. Bushman, International Human Press, August 3, 2014. Reprinted by permission.

As you read, consider the following questions:

1. What three reasons does Dr. Bushman give for why he considers playing violent video games more harmful than watching violent TV programs or films?
2. In what two ways do people believe violent games can be good for you?
3. What are the four reasons why most people deny that violent video games have harmful effects?

I n 1972, the Surgeon General issued the following warning on violent TV programs: "It is clear to me that the causal relationship between televised violence and antisocial behavior is sufficient to warrant appropriate and immediate remedial action. ... There comes a time when the data are sufficient to justify action. That time has come." (Steinfeld, 1972).

That was over 4 decades ago! In the years since this Surgeon General warning was issued, hundreds of additional studies have shown a link between violent media exposure and aggression (e.g., Anderson & Bushman, 2002a). The Surgeon General warning was about violent TV programs and films. What about violent video games?

Are Violent Video Games More Harmful than Violent TV Programs and Films?

There are at least three reasons to believe that violent video games might be even more harmful than violent TV programs and films.

- First, video game play is active whereas watching TV is passive. People learn better when they are actively involved. Suppose you wanted to learn how to fly an airplane. What would be the best method to use: read a book, watch a TV program, or use a video game flight simulator?
- Second, players of violent video games are more likely to identify with a violent character. If the game is a first person

shooter, players have the same visual perspective as the killer. If the game is third person, the player controls the actions of the violent character from a more distant visual perspective. In a violent TV program, viewers might or might not identify with a violent character. People are more likely to behave aggressively themselves when they identify with a violent character (e.g., Konijn et al., 2007)

- Third, violent games directly reward violent behavior, such as by awarding points or by allowing players to advance to the next game level. In some games, players are rewarded through verbal praise, such as hearing the words "Nice shot!" after killing an enemy. It is well known that rewarding behavior increases its frequency. (Would you go to work tomorrow if your boss said you would no longer be paid?) In TV programs, reward is not directly tied to the viewer's behavior.

In summary, there are good theoretical reasons to believe that violent video games are even more harmful that violent TV programs or films. We also have empirical data showing this (Polman et al., 2008). In this study, children were randomly assigned to play a violent video game or watch someone else play it. There was also a nonviolent video game control condition. The results showed that boys who played a violent video game were more aggressive afterwards than were boys who merely watched.

Are Violent Video Games Good For You?

Some people claim that violent video games are good for you. Some players believe that violent video games are cathartic (i.e., they allow players to release pent up anger into harmless channels). The scientific evidence directly contradicts this idea. Over 130 studies have been conducted on over 130,000 participants around the world (Anderson et al., 2010). These studies show that violent video games increase aggressive thoughts, angry feelings, physiological arousal (e.g., heart rate, blood pressure), and aggressive behavior. Violent games also decrease helping behavior and feelings of empathy for others.

Other people claim that playing violent games increases eye-hand coordination, and research supports this claim (e.g., Green & Bavelier, 2007). However, violent content might not be required to obtain these beneficial effects. Perhaps similar video games without violence would also increase eye-hand coordination.

Why Do People Deny the Harmful Effects of Violent Video Games?

Although the scientific evidence clearly shows that violent video games have harmful effects, many people still deny these effects, especially violent game players. There are at least four reasons why.

- First, people may think: "I play violent video games and I've never killed anyone." This fallacious reasoning is a good example of how the "availability heuristic" coupled with the "base rate problem" (Kahneman & Tversky, 1973) distort reasoning. People have great difficulty judging influences on events when the base rate probability of the event is very low. It is not surprising that people who play violent video games have not killed anyone because very few people kill anyone. For example, fewer than 6 people per 100,000 are murdered each year in the United States (U.S. Federal Bureau of Investigation, 2010). It is very difficult to predict rare events, such as murder, using exposure to violent video games or any other factor. However, murder is the most salient violent event to most people; so when they don't have "available" in memory cases of people playing violent games and then murdering, they ignore the base rate of murder and conclude that violent games have no effect on aggression.
- Second, researchers have also found that people believe the media have a much stronger effect on others than on themselves. This effect is very robust and is called the third person effect (e.g., Davison, 1983). The consequence of this psychological effect is that people may often agree that media violence has a bad effect on some people, but not on

themselves. This thinking then leads to a denial of the overall importance of the effects from a public health standpoint.

- Third, the entertainment industry frequently claims that violent media do not increase aggression (Anderson & Bushman 2002b). Even though the public may recognize that making such claims is in the economic self-interest of the entertainment industry, the repetition of the claims of no effects still seems to have an effect. Since the 1972 Surgeon General warning, the scientific evidence has grown even stronger. But an analysis of over 600 news reports shows that over time, news stories are more likely to deny the harmful effect of media violence. Most Americans aren't even aware that the U.S. Surgeon General issued a warning about TV violence. Perhaps this is because most Americans get their information from the mass media. The entertainment industry is probably reluctant to admit that they are marketing a harmful product, much like the tobacco industry was reluctant to admit that they were marketing a harmful product.

- Fourth, people do not understand psychological processes as well as they understand biological processes. If you see a violent video game player assault another person, it is difficult to know the direct cause of the assault. Was it playing violent video games for hours on end, or was it something else? The psychological process by which playing violent video games produces this result is not as intuitive to most people as are biological processes. People are probably more accepting of the idea that smoking causes lung cancer, for example, because it is much easier to grasp the idea that smoke going into the lungs, damages cells, and starts tumor growth.

These processes combine to create an atmosphere in which non-expert journalists, and even some social scientists, write articles and books arguing that violent video games are not harmful. However, the vast majority of social scientists working in the area believe that violent video games can be harmful (e.g., Pollard Sacks, Bushman, & Anderson, 2011).

References

Anderson, C. A., & Bushman, B. J. (2002a). Media violence and societal violence. Science, 295, 2377-2378.

Anderson, C. A., & Bushman, B. J. (2002b). Media violence and the American Public revisited. American Psychologist, 57, 448-450.

Davison, W. P. (1983). The third-person effect in communication. Public Opinion Quarterly, 47, 1-15.

Kahneman, D., & Tversky, A. (1973). On the psychology of prediction. Psychological Review, 80, 237–251.

Pollard Sacks, D., Bushman, B. J., & Anderson, C. A. (2011). Do violent video games harm children? Comparing the scientific amicus curiae "experts" in Brown v. Entertainment Merchants Association. Northwestern University Law Review: Colloquy, 106, 1-12. http://colloquy.law.northwestern.edu/main/2011/05/do-violent-video-games-harm-children-comparing-the-scientific-amicus-curiae-experts-in-brown-v-cnter.html

Steinfeld, J. (1972). Statement in hearings before Subcommittee on Communications of Committee on Commerce (United States Senate, Serial #92-52, pp. 25–27). Washington, DC: U.S. Government Printing Office.

> *"Videogames are (once again) being used as a scapegoat by politicians looking for a simple answer to causes of violence. But despite how they skew research outcomes there is one undeniable fact: aggression is a normal response that is caused by many different triggers."*

Violent Video Games Aren't Necessarily the Cause of Aggressive Behavior

Michael Kasumovic

In the following viewpoint, Michael Kasumovic brings up several other triggers besides violent video games that cause aggressive behavior and contends that these other triggers are not necessarily considered in the studies that declare the games as cause. Historically, confrontational scenarios commonly produce aggressive behavior. In other words, it's in our genes. But the question he raises is, does an aggressive response determine that a person is violent? There are much bigger issues at play that have a greater effect on violent behavior than playing violent video games. Kasumovic is a lecturer and ARC DECRA fellow who does research on evolution and behavior for the Australian Research Council.

"Violent Videogames Aren't the Problem—It's in Our Genes," by Michael Kasumovic, The Conversation, February 8, 2013. https://theconversation.com/violent-videogames-arent-the-problem-its-in-our-genes-12064. Licensed Under CC BY-ND 4.0.

As you read this article, consider the following questions:

1. Besides sporting events, what three other things increase aggression in people?
2. What two social factors have a greater effect on adolescent aggression than violent video games?
3. Instead of politicians, who does Mr. Kasumovic think should examine the effects of video games on children and adults?

T he debate around videogames and violence is getting seriously out of control—not least in the US. Just take this recent homepage on the *Huffington Post*:

'VIDEO GAMES ARE A BIGGER PROBLEM THAN GUNS!' GOP Senator: Blame 'Call of Duty'… 'Six Bullets Might Not Be Enough'… Female Gun Advocate: Assault Weapons Give Young Mothers 'Peace of Mind' … NRA Chief: Background Checks Hurt 'The Little Guy' … SENATORS WHINE: We Can't Bring Guns To Hearing

Hyperbole aside, videogames are (once again) being used as a scapegoat by politicians looking for a simple answer to causes of violence. But despite how they skew research outcomes there is one undeniable fact: aggression is a normal response that is caused by many different triggers.

The US Senate, along with the media, is in a large debate over whether aggression caused from videogames does or does not cause violence.

Jason Schreier, a writer at Kotaku, published an excellent article recently summarising what researchers have found about links between videogames, aggression and violence over the last 20 years. If you haven't yet, I urge you to read it.

It highlights points for and against links between videogames and violence. But as with all other articles discussing the topic, it focuses on videogames and aggression—and therein lies the problem.

There's no reason to believe the aggression video games cause is any different or more severe than aggression from any other source.

A violent evolution

Let's look at aggression from an evolutionary standpoint. Humans have long since responded aggressively when in competition, territorial disputes and disagreements, as doing so could provide an advantage. Throughout our development, individuals that responded aggressively in the proper contexts would have had more favourable outcomes, and therefore access to greater resources and mating opportunities.

In the same vein, one can see how too much aggression could be negative. Express this aggression at the improper time, or allow it to escalate, and you could find yourself in a potentially dire and/ or life-threatening situation—clearly something natural selection would select against.

As a result of the above, individuals responding moderately and at the right times may have had the best success.

Although most individuals no longer encounter the same types of situations that require the aggressive responses of our predecessors, the physiological machinery remains and responds to situations that mimic historical confrontational challenges.

Sporting events increase aggression, especially when teams are more equally matched, and workplace aggression seems to be caused, with alarming regularity, by belligerent supervisors.

Increased alcohol use and hot weather, among many other triggers, can likewise make us aggressive.

So should we be surprised that videogames can increase aggression? I don't think so. But we should be able to scrutinise this link more closely to ask whether video games make us more aggressive than other triggers and whether this aggression persists for longer.

Putting a finger on the trigger

Unfortunately, studies don't often compare responses between different aggressive triggers (although the outcomes may be similar) and we don't understand how aggression caused by video games compares to other aggressive triggers. But we do have some insight into the duration of aggressive behaviours and thoughts after playing violent video games.

Research suggests it can be less than ten minutes. It's been estimated this timeframe can be increased by 24 hours if players dwell on the game: a common outcome when individuals continually reflect on what triggered the aggression in the first place.

As a result, it's possible excessive gameplay could affect aggression over the long term. Studies looking for exactly that link do find effects of violent video games on long-term aggressive behaviour.

But when researchers consider other social factors linked to adolescent aggression, it seems increased exposure to family violence and negative peer influences and less communication with their parents have greater effects. Violent video games, it seems, may be an indicator, but there are clearly deeper issues at play.

Experimenting with aggression

I'd like you to imagine you're driving your car, calmly, alone. As you're cruising along, a car comes squealing by and cuts you off, meaning you have to swerve to avoid it as it speeds away. If at that very moment you had a button in your car that would blast the driver with some of the most annoying sounds possible, would you press the button? And if so, how loud would you blast it?

This is an example of how studies examine the effect violent and non-violent video games have on aggression. Two individuals play a game, and the loser receives an offensive noise blast. In general, studies show that individuals playing violent games tend to blast opponents with a louder noise.

There are other means to test aggression, such as word association or even hot sauce, but the point is that a pre-determined punishment is often used to assess aggression at that exact moment.

Let's take a step back and look at this experimental design in a different light. Participants play a competitive game to determine which individual is better. Should we be surprised that individuals become aggressive in this scenario?

In many animals (humans included), winners often perform "victory displays"—a well-known behaviour used to reinforce a triumph. As the only way for opponents to communicate in the type of experiments mentioned above is through pre-determined punishments, the noise blast (or its equivalent) could perhaps be viewed as a dominance or victory display.

In such situations, does responding in an aggressive way make you a violent individual? Unlikely, as aggressive feelings will likely dissipate after time, as in the videogame study.

There are, of course, some individuals that do respond violently in certain situations. If we use driving as an example again, we've all heard of stories where road rage escalates into violence.

In such situations, it's important to remember that these individuals may perceive and react to aggression differently. This doesn't make their violent response acceptable, but does encourage us to try to understand why this variation exists. This is where it may be especially fruitful to combine evolutionary and psychological approaches that could help explain the variation in these responses.

In the same way, there may be a subset of individuals that are at a greater risk of the influence of violent video games. As video games have many benefits, rather than demonising them, shouldn't we use video games to try and identify these individuals?

Unfortunately, I doubt the $10 million the US president pledged towards video game research will examine that.

What needs to be done

The debate is already hijacked by rich, old, white politicians that are clearly misguided through outdated morals and NRA donations. But the biggest problem is the xenophobia about societal progression.

The introduction to the the book *Grand Theft Childhood* by Lawrence Kutner and Cheryl Olson provides an excellent historical overview of how politicians have responded correspondingly to each introduction of new media starting from the dime novels of the late 19th century, to silent films, to movies and videogames today.

What's needed is a lobby group as powerful as the NRA that stands up for gamers, and not the industry. Gamers make up a large proportion of today's population and if each of them were card-carrying members of an organisation that critically and honestly examined the effects of video games on children and adults, we might be able to have a proper discussion about their benefits and costs.

I'm sure gamers wouldn't disagree with the idea, especially given that many of us are parents and have our own children's safety in mind.

"Even if you account for the child's sex, age, race, the age they were first referred to juvenile court—which is a very powerful effect—and a bunch of other media effects, like screen time and exposure. Even with all of that, the video game measure still mattered."

Violent Video Games Are a Risk Factor for Youth Violence

Iowa State University News Service

In the following viewpoint, researchers at Iowa State University interpret the results of a study that showed a strong connection between violent video games and youth violence. While exposure to violent gaming was not the sole cause of violent behavior, the study showed that it was indeed a risk factor. Frequency of play and an affinity for violent games, the authors argue, demonstrated a strong connection to delinquency and violent behavior. This study was conducted by researchers at Iowa State University.

As you read, consider the following questions:

1. What kinds of violent acts had the 227 juvenile offenders involved in this study committed?
2. What does Dr. Gentile recommend that people consider when studying serious aggression?
3. What do the researchers say is the takeaway for parents?

People are quick to point the finger or dismiss the effect of violent video games as a factor in criminal behavior. New evidence from Iowa State researchers demonstrates a link between video games and youth violence and delinquency.

Matt DeLisi, a professor of sociology, said the research shows a strong connection even when controlling for a history of violence and psychopathic traits among juvenile offenders.

"When critics say, 'Well, it's probably not video games, it's probably how antisocial they are,' we can address that directly because we controlled for a lot of things that we know matter," DeLisi said. "Even if you account for the child's sex, age, race, the age they were first referred to juvenile court—which is a very powerful effect—and a bunch of other media effects, like screen time and exposure. Even with all of that, the video game measure still mattered."

The results were not unexpected, but somewhat surprising for Douglas Gentile, an associate professor of psychology, who has studied the effects of video game violence exposure and minor aggression, like hitting, teasing and name-calling.

"I didn't expect to see much of an effect when we got to serious delinquent and criminal level aggression because youth who commit that level of aggression have a lot of things going wrong for them. They often have a lot of risk factors and very few protective factors in their lives," Gentile said.

The study published in the April issue of *Youth Violence and Juvenile Justice* examined the level of video game exposure for 227 juvenile offenders in Pennsylvania. The average offender had committed nearly nine serious acts of violence, such as gang fighting, hitting a parent or attacking another person in the prior year.

The results show that both the frequency of play and affinity for violent games were strongly associated with delinquent and violent behavior. Craig Anderson, Distinguished Professor of psychology and director of the Center for the Study of Violence at Iowa State, said violent video game exposure is not the sole cause of violence, but this study shows it is a risk factor.

"Can we say from this study that Adam Lanza, or any of the others, went off and killed people because of media violence? You can't take the stand of the NRA that it's strictly video games and not guns," Anderson said. "You also can't take the stand of the entertainment industry that it has nothing to do with media violence that it's all about guns and not about media violence. They're both wrong and they're both right, both are causal risk factors."

Researchers point out that juvenile offenders have several risk factors that influence their behavior. The next step is to build on this research to determine what combination of factors is the most volatile and if there is a saturation point.

"When studying serious aggression, looking at multiple risk factors matters more than looking at any one," Gentile said. "The cutting edge of research is trying to understand in what combination do the individual risk factors start influencing each other in ways to either enhance or mitigate the odds of aggression?"

What does this mean for parents?

There is a lot of misinformation about video game exposure, Anderson said, that makes it difficult for parents to understand the harmful effects. Although it is one variable that parents can control, he understands that with mixed messages about the risks some parents may feel it's not worth the effort.

"What parent would go through the pain and all the effort it takes to really control their child's media diet, if they don't really think it makes any difference? That is why it is so important to get out the simple and clear message that media violence does matter," Anderson said.

Just because a child plays a violent video game does not mean he or she is going to act violently. Researchers say if there is a take away for parents, it is an awareness of what their children are playing and how that may influence their behavior.

"I think parents need to be truthful and honest about who their children are in terms of their psychiatric functioning," DeLisi said. "If you have a kid who is antisocial, who is a little bit vulnerable to influence, giving them something that allows them to escape into themselves for a long period of time isn't a healthy thing."

> *"So what am I feeling when I'm killing in video games? What emotions do I experience when taking the life of either an artificially-intelligent character, or the avatar of a rival human player who would probably kill me first if I weren't quicker on the draw? In a word? Fun. That's it."*

Playing Video Games Does Not Cause Violence

Matt Terzi

In the following viewpoint, Matt Terzi tackles the connection between violent video games and aggression from a personal perspective. As someone who has been playing video games since he was a child, Terzi asserts that video games do not cause violence. He, along with 200 academics, have signed a letter refuting the findings of the American Psychological Society (APA), which claim that violent video games are a contributing factor to violent behavior. Terzi believes that the games are purely entertainment—action-packed thrillers that drop a person into the action the way that movies can't and are, for the most part, simply harmless fun. Terzi is a political satirist and essayist from Binghamton, New York.

As you read, consider the following questions:

1. What kind of person does Mr. Terzi say he is, despite the fact that he has killed billions of virtual people over the years in video games?

2. What did he learn from the torture scene in *Grand Theft Auto V*?

3. What does he recommend to people who think violent video games cause violent behavior and what does he believe will be the result?

A recent study conducted by the American Psychological Society claims that violent video games can be a contributing factor toward violent behavior. But now, more than 200 academics have signed an open letter lambasting that report's findings. And as a person who has been playing video games since my early childhood, I'd like to add my voice to that group as well. I can confidently state this as an empirical fact: video games do not cause violent behavior. And I have a lifetime of experiences to support that.

Since my very early childhood, with the Atari 2600 and IBM PC Jr., I've played countless games, mostly on PC, but also on a large number of consoles. My parents always made sure we had the newest game consoles, and my Dad working for IBM meant we always had the latest and greatest personal computers. This was long before the days of Facebook or goofy cat videos on YouTube. Gaming was just about the only thing a kid could do on a PC in the 1980's. It was that or spreadsheets. I think games win that debate. I was hooked on gaming at a very early age, and even today, in my thirties, gaming constitutes a pretty significant chunk of my leisure time.

If you count my overzealous use of nuclear weapons in the *Civilization* franchise, I've easily killed tens of billions of nameless virtual people in all those years of gaming. I've played every violent game you can think of, and have done well (and by "done well,"

I mean I've killed lots and lots of virtual people) in almost every one of them. *Doom*, *Postal*, the *Battlefield* franchise, every *Grand Theft Auto* game ever made… I've raked up terrifying death counts in them all.

Despite those billions of (mostly senseless) murders in video games, I'm one of the least violent people you'll likely encounter. I'm a big liberal softy who does not and would never own a gun. I'm not a big fan of real-life war and have taken part in numerous protests over the years to end it. I support President Obama's Iran deal and see it as the only feasible option for conflict resolution; bombing Iran will solve nothing. Being an advocate for real-world peace and a virtual killing machine in the video game realm are not mutually exclusive.

So what am I feeling when I'm killing in video games? What emotions do I experience when taking the life of either an artificially-intelligent character, or the avatar of a rival human player who would probably kill me first if I weren't quicker on the draw? In a word? Fun. That's it.

Imagine the thrill of taking off in a fighter jet from an aircraft carrier and dogfighting with a dozen other planes. You eventually take too much damage, though, and your engine starts to stall and flame out. You eject, landing in the middle of a warzone, where you quickly draw your pistol and jump into a whole new fight. Video games are exhilarating, action-packed thrillers that drop you into the action in nonlinear ways that movies and books simply can't.

That's not to say there haven't been moments where I felt utterly disturbed by what I was doing in these games. I played through the famous, gruesomely upsetting torture scene In *Grand Theft Auto V*, where you, playing as the instantly-legendary character Trevor Phillips, violently torture another character. It was the most grotesque thing I'd ever encountered in a video game. But it certainly wouldn't inspire me to torture another person … far from it. If anything, it helped me better appreciate just how horrible torture is and show me, in graphic detail, precisely why torture is an archaic device of untold evil. You aren't supposed to have "fun" torturing that man … it's supposed to make you feel disgusted and violated. And of all my countless gamer friends, I don't know a single player who didn't feel exactly that.

Video games are the most profitable form of entertainment in the world today, bringing in vastly more money than book sales and movie sales combined. Over 1.4 billion people the world over are playing games. We spend 3 billion hours each week playing them. Despite that gruesome aforementioned torture scene, *Grand Theft Auto V* has sold nearly 52 million copies worldwide, making it the best-selling video game of all time. How many of those 52 million gamers are going to run out and kill another person? Statistically, not very many.

If you think video games cause violence, there's only one thing I can really recommend for you to do: actually play a video game. Pick a game of any genre that interests you and give it a spin. If you hate it, you can always give it to someone else, but chances are you're going to quickly discover that these games do not promote violence. If anything, they really discourage it. But until you actually try one of these games, your opinion, like the cake, is a lie.

Video games are an art form, and like films and books before the medium, gaming is starting to truly develop its own voice. If you think a game is too violent, don't play it. If you think your child can't handle a game's content, be a good parent like mine were and get involved in your child's gaming activities, or shield them from that content entirely if you feel that's the best methodology to deploy. But until you've actually played these games, please don't pass judgment on those of us who have. And for the love of God, don't try to force these games to change because you, a person who will never play them, take issue with their content. You might be behind the curve on gaming, but that doesn't give you a right to tell me or anyone else what we should consider safe, harmless fun.

> *"Finding that a young man who committed a violent crime also played a popular video game [...] is as pointless as pointing out that the criminal also wore socks."*

Violent Video Games Don't Lead to Increases in Crime Rates

Eddie Makuch

In the following viewpoint Eddie Makuch cites a study, Violent Video Games and Real-World Violence: Rhetoric Versus Data, *conducted by researchers at Villanova University and Rutgers University, that analyzed how popular video game trends, such as video game sales, compared to real-world crime rates. Makuch argues that he results of this study showed no evidence of a correlation between the games and crime rates and challenges one of the study's authors, in an interview. Makuch is a news editor at GameSpot.*

As you read, consider the following questions:

1. What other trends besides sales were considered for this study?
2. What reason did Patrick Markey speculate for the possibility that playing violent video games might be related to decreases in violent crime?
3. What did the research show in respect to changes in violence when new game consoles or more realistic graphics have been introduced?

The effect violent video games have on real-world behavior has long been a hotly debated topic. Some argue there is assuredly a link between playing violent video games and increased levels of aggressive behavior, while others maintain that games themselves don't cause violence, but are rather one prominent risk factor for violent real-world behavior. Now, another study has been published, this one claiming that there is no evidence to support the notion that violent video games lead to increases in real-world violent crimes.

The study, *Violent Video Games and Real-World Violence: Rhetoric Versus Data*, was conducted by researchers at Villanova University and Rutgers University, and was published recently in the *Psychology of Popular Media Culture*. Through four unique data analyses, the researchers looked at how popular video game trends, like annual and monthly video game sales, as well as Google Trends keyword search volume, compared to real-world crime rates.

What the researchers found surprised them. If it's true what some researchers are saying, that playing violent video games might lead to increases in real-world violence, you would expect this new study to bear that out. But it was not the case. In fact, the research showed that there is no evidence that violent video games are positively correlated to real-world crime rates in the United States.

Need the short version? The research is summed up thusly:

"Annual trends in video game sales for the past 33 years were unrelated to violent crime both concurrently and up to four years later. Unexpectedly, monthly sales of video games were related to concurrent decreases in aggravated assaults and were unrelated to homicides. Searches for violent video game walkthroughs and guides were also related to decreases in aggravated assaults and homicides two months later. Finally, homicides tended to decrease in the months following the release of popular M-rated violent video games."

"Finding that a young man who committed a violent crime also played a popular video game, such as *Call of Duty*, *Halo*, or *Grand Theft Auto*, is as pointless as pointing out that the criminal also wore socks."

It's a fascinating finding, even if it does have some limitations (like most major studies). I recently had the chance to speak with one of its authors, Patrick Markey, an associate professor of psychology at Villanova. You can read the study for yourself here, and see my full conversation with Markey below.

What inspired you to launch into this research in the first place?

Many people in the media and even my fellow researchers have linked violent video games and other forms of media to real acts of horrific violence. For example, in testimony before the U.S. Senate Dr. Craig Anderson argued that '... high exposure to media violence is a major contributing cause of the high rate of violence in modern U.S. society.' More recently, in the pages of Pediatrics Dr. Strasburger claimed that '.. an estimated 10% to 30% of violence in society can be attributed to the impact of media violence.' However, these statements are based on research that has not actually examined serious acts of violence—most previous studies either examined proxy assessments of aggression—giving a person spicy hot sauce, exposing a person to an irritating noise—or self-reports of hostility. We wanted to see whether such findings generalize to homicide and aggravated assault rates.

Do Violent Video Games Decrease Criminal Activity?

High sales of violent video games do not result in spikes in crime rates, instead correlating with a decrease in violent youth activity, according to research statistics shared in the *New York Times*.

According to the *Times*, between 1994 and 2010 the number of violent crimes among youth offenders fell by more than half, to 224 crimes per population of 100,000. At the same time, sales of video games have more than doubled since 1996.

In a working paper published online by a group of economists from three universities, weekly sales of violent video games were monitored across several different communities. The study found that both violent occurrences and high video game sales are seasonal; violence peaks in summer while more video games are sold during the holiday season. The group analyzed data from communities like college towns with high youth populations, monitoring crime rates in the month following high game sales.

According to University of Texas at Arlington economist Dr. Michael Ward, one of the study's authors, high violent video game sales were related to a decrease in violent crime rates.

"We found that higher rates of violent video game sales related to a decrease in crimes, and especially violent crimes," he said.

"Violent video game sales coincide with drop in violent youth crimes, according to study," by Alexa Ray, Vox Media, February 13 2013.

Your research shows there is no evidence to support a link between violent video games and real-world violent crime in the US—do you think you'd find similar results in other regions?

There is no reason to believe the effects would be any different. However, this is an empirical question and we hope future researchers might consider examining it.

What were some of the most surprising findings of your research?

By far the most surprising finding was that violent video games were negatively related to aggravated assault and homicides. This really surprised me. However, after this discovery we replicated this finding examining violent movies. It turns out, like violent video games, the popularity of violent films is inversely related to violent crime.

It seems to me like a major limitation of this study is that it only accounts for one risk factor for violent behavior—violent video games. What's your response to this?

Obviously correlation does not imply causation so one needs to always be cautious when interpreting ecological data—this same issue applies to whether we are examining links between autism and vaccines or smoking and lung cancer. However, in this study we did not simply look at the relations between violent video games and crime. We also accounted for various trends in the data which might explain this relationship. For example, we eliminated seasonal trends which remove any extraneous results which might have occurred because video game sales tend to be high in the winter and crime tends to be high in the summer. We also removed linear trends which might occur if violent crime is generally going down and video game sales are generally increasing. We also examined various predictors (video game sales, searches for violent video games, release dates of violent video games) both annually and monthly. Even with all these issues considered the same result emerged—violent video games were negatively related to violent crime.

Why did you decide to conduct your study using the methods that you did? What other possibilities were considered?

Ecological studies, like this one, are probably the best way to examine events like homicides. Such a—fortunately—rare behavior cannot really be studied in the laboratory.

Some of your results suggest that there is actually a decrease in violent crime in response to violent video games; are you saying here that playing violent games might potentially make the world a safer place?

This is where we need to be careful—otherwise, we run the risk of being sensationalistic. I think the biggest 'take home' of this study is that violent video games were not related to increases in violent crime—not even a little. However, if we assume that violent video games are actually related to decreases in violent crime, we can speculate about why this might have occurred. It is possible that violent media might reduce severe acts of violence because it effectively removes violent individuals from other social venues where they might have otherwise committed a violent act. In other words, violent individuals might attend a movie, watch television, or play a video game instead of engaging in other activities—going to a bar, socializing on the streets—that are more likely to result in a violent altercation.

Was it difficult for you when conducting this study to separate, as you say, scientific results from scientific conjecture? How did you overcome that?

As scientists—and reporters—we need to use caution when generalizing results from laboratories and questionnaires to things like violent crime rates. In a similar manner, restraint is warranted when research collected in university laboratories is used to explain the idiosyncratic behavior of a specific individual—e.g., the Aurora, Colorado shooter, James Holmes. Given that the public, media, and lawmakers tend to be concerned about trends in violent behavior and specific acts of violence, it is understandable why some researchers might be tempted to make sensationalistic claims based only on laboratory and questionnaire research. However, it is important for us, as researchers, to be aware of the tentative nature of such claims and consistently acknowledge these limitations.

Your study is not the first to reach this conclusion, yet video games continue to be singled out as movies, books, and other mediums are often overlooked in the popular discussion on the role violent video games might have on behavior. Why do you think this is?

There is no evidence that, even in the laboratory, violent video games have a different effect on mundane acts of aggression than other forms of violent media—the 'effect sizes' found in studies are similar regardless of the media examined. However, you are correct that violent video games are always the focus. Probably the best explanation for this is what Dr. Chris Ferguson calls a 'Moral Panic.' That is, people who are the leaders of a society often blame things which they do not value for societal ills.

In the wake of the Sandy Hook shooting, many lawmakers proposed new measures against violent video games, though none have really panned out. What effect do you think your research could have on future legislative action?

As a researcher my job is to present the science and let others figure out what should be done with it. My hope is simply that others consider these data whenever a person suggests violent video games are 'a major contributing cause of the high rate of violence in modern U.S. society,' or that 'an estimated 10% to 30% of violence in society can be attributed to the impact of media violence.'

As I understand it, your study was conducted prior to the arrival of the Xbox One and PlayStation 4, new consoles from Microsoft and Sony that offer better graphics than their predecessors. Do you think that as time goes on and games become far more life-like and fully realized, we could see a different trend than the one you observed?

During each new generation of game consoles there has not been a noticeable change in violence. Additionally, research in laboratories has not found that more 'realistic' graphics have bigger effects of even mundane acts of aggression. So it is unlikely the next generation will alter the trends observed in the study.

What are you looking at for further research on this topic?

No idea—maybe your suggestion about looking at different countries.

You have been studying games and violence for a long time now. Over the course of those years, how has your perception of the video game industry shifted?

I don't really have a strong opinion about the game industry itself. They make a product and my job is basically to figure out if that product might be harmful. However, I do hope results from studies like ours will cause researchers to reevaluate their previously held beliefs about violent video games. After all, we all want pretty much the same thing. We want to uncover the 'truth.' We want science, not sensationalism, to inform policies concerning violent video games. We want to protect others from any threats posed by violent video games, but we do not want violent video games to distract from the more important causes of horrific acts of violence.

Periodical and Internet Sources Bibliography

The following articles have been selected to supplement the diverse views presented in this chapter.

Giovanni Albanese, Jr., "Violent Video Games Create Aggression, but Do They Cause Kids to Commit Crimes?" *Healthline*, August 14, 2015.

Dave Anderson, "10 Reasons Violent Video Games Contribute to Youth Violence," *Listland,* March 30, 2016.

Maeve Duggan, "Games and Gamers," *Pew Research Center,* December 15, 2015.

Zaid Jilani "Study: Playing Violent Video Games Might Actually Make Us LESS Violent," *Alternet*, October 1 2014.

Erik Kain, "As Video Game Sales Climb Year Over Year, Violent Crime Continues to Fall," *Forbes*, April 19, 2012.

Krista Lofgren, "2016 Video Game Statistics & Trends Who's Playing What and Why?" *BigFish Games*, February 8, 2016.

Luca Milani et al., "Violent Video Games and Children's Aggressive Behaviors," *Sage Journals,* August 5, 2015.

Dan Pearson, "APA study established violent games as 'risk factor' for violent behaviour," *GamesIndustry.biz*, August 14, 2015.

Alexandra Siffirlin, "Violent Video Games are Linked to Aggression, Study Says," Time, August 17, 2015.

Margaret Weigel, "The contested field of violent video games: Research Roundup," *Journalist's Resource*, January 31, 2015.

OPPOSING
VIEWPOINTS®
SERIES

What Is the Effect of Violent Video Games on Health and Development?

Chapter Preface

What kinds of effects do violent games have on our psyches and emotions? Do they make us more or less empathetic? Desensitize us to violence? Stress us out or relieve stress? Blur the lines between reality and fantasy? Or are they just a fun pastime?

A multitude of studies have addressed parental concerns about gamers becoming less empathetic and/or games desensitizing them to violence. The studies test physical variables, such as heart rate increases and changes in brain activity and connect these changes to empathetic response. Others examine emotional responses and many agree that playing violent games for long periods of time can have a detrimental effect. But some of the studies show the opposite effect: that children learn empathy by being part of violent actions that teach them right from wrong or show them what it's like to walk in the shoes of someone who is a victim of violence.

Stress is another factor that has been examined in relation to video game-playing. One study found that 61.9% of boys played the games to relax, others to work through their anger. Is this just another venue for kids to relieve stress and have fun, like wrestling with one another, or playing active, physical games? Or, as other studies have found, do kids experience high levels of stress during games where someone is trying to kill them, and thus act out with aggression following the game?

Finally, some argue that playing violent games causes people to blur the lines between reality and fantasy. They cite games like *EverQuest*, to which some kids have become addicted, and have had trouble returning to reality from their intense immersion in the game. Or the case of 16-year-old Evan Ramsey, who shot and killed two people in Bethel, Alaska. He claimed that he didn't realize shooting a gun would actually kill someone, because in the video games he played, if he shot somebody, they would get back up. However, are all the other factors surrounding these kids, such as family situations, mental health, or problems at school taken into consideration? Is it immersion in the games that's the problem, pre-existing mental health issues, or a combination of both?

Yet, with 97% of teens in America playing video games, it would seem that the majority of them are not addicted, nor do they live in a fantasy world from which they can't emerge. For most of them, the games are simply that: just games.

In the following chapter, the authors address the issue of violent video games as they relate to empathy, desensitization, stress, and distinguishing reality from fantasy.

| "It appears that individuals who play violent video games habituate or 'get used to' all the violence and eventually become physiologically numb to it."

Research Shows Violent Video Games Reduce Emotional Reactivity

Craig Anderson

In the following viewpoint, Craig Anderson and Nicholas Camagey conducted a study to determine if exposure to violent video games caused a decrease in sensitivity and helpful behavior to others. They measured different physiological responses following game-playing while participants watched real-life scenes of violent behavior. They found that there was a lower response to violence by the participants who had played violent games as opposed to those who had played non-violent ones; their conclusion is that "the entertainment media landscape could accurately be described as an effective systematic violence desensitization tool." Anderson is professor of psychology at Iowa State University.

"ISU Psychologists Produce First Study On Violence Desensitization from Video Games," by Craig Anderson, Iowa State University of Science and Technology, July 24, 2006. Reprinted by permission.

As you read, consider the following questions:

1. How do the authors of the study define desensitization to violence?
2. What methodology did the researches use to measure desensitization?
3. What different reactions were found by participants playing violent and non-violent games when they were exposed to scenes of real violence?

Research led by a pair of Iowa State University psychologists has proven for the first time that exposure to violent video games can desensitize individuals to real-life violence.

Nicholas Carnagey, an Iowa State psychology instructor and research assistant, and ISU Distinguished Professor of Psychology Craig Anderson collaborated on the study with Brad Bushman, a former Iowa State psychology professor now at the University of Michigan, and Vrije Universiteit, Amsterdam.

They authored a paper titled "The Effects of Video Game Violence on Physiological Desensitization to Real-Life Violence," which was published in the current issue of the *Journal of Experimental Social Psychology*. In this paper, the authors define desensitization to violence as "a reduction in emotion-related physiological reactivity to real violence."

Their paper reports that past research—including their own studies—documents that exposure to violent video games increases aggressive thoughts, angry feelings, physiological arousal and aggressive behaviors, and decreases helpful behaviors. Previous studies also found that more than 85 percent of video games contain some violence, and approximately half of video games include serious violent actions.

The methodology

Their latest study tested 257 college students (124 men and 133 women) individually. After taking baseline physiological measurements on heart rate and galvanic skin response—and asking questions to control for their preference for violent video games and general aggression—participants played one of eight randomly assigned violent or non-violent video games for 20 minutes. The four violent video games were *Carmageddon, Duke Nukem, Mortal Kombat* or *Future Cop*; the non-violent games were *Glider Pro, 3D Pinball, 3D Munch Man* and *Tetra Madness*.

After playing a video game, a second set of five-minute heart rate and skin response measurements were taken. Participants were then asked to watch a 10-minute videotape of actual violent episodes taken from TV programs and commercially-released films in the following four contexts: courtroom outbursts, police confrontations, shootings and prison fights. Heart rate and skin response were monitored throughout the viewing.

The physical differences

When viewing real violence, participants who had played a violent video game experienced skin response measurements significantly lower than those who had played a non-violent video game. The participants in the violent video game group also had lower heart rates while viewing the real-life violence compared to the nonviolent video game group.

"The results demonstrate that playing violent video games, even for just 20 minutes, can cause people to become less physiologically aroused by real violence," said Carnagey. "Participants randomly assigned to play a violent video game had relatively lower heart rates and galvanic skin responses while watching footage of people being beaten, stabbed and shot than did those randomly assigned to play nonviolent video games.

"It appears that individuals who play violent video games habituate or 'get used to' all the violence and eventually become physiologically numb to it."

Participants in the violent versus non-violent games conditions did not differ in heart rate or skin response at the beginning of the study, or immediately after playing their assigned game. However, their physiological reactions to the scenes of real violence did differ significantly, a result of having just played a violent or a non-violent game. The researchers also controlled for trait aggression and preference for violent video games.

The researchers' conclusion

They conclude that the existing video game rating system, the content of much entertainment media, and the marketing of those media combine to produce "a powerful desensitization intervention on a global level."

"It (marketing of video game media) initially is packaged in ways that are not too threatening, with cute cartoon-like characters, a total absence of blood and gore, and other features that make the overall experience a pleasant one," said Anderson. "That arouses positive emotional reactions that are incongruent with normal negative reactions to violence. Older children consume increasingly threatening and realistic violence, but the increases are gradual and always in a way that is fun.

"In short, the modern entertainment media landscape could accurately be described as an effective systematic violence desensitization tool," he said. "Whether modern societies want this to continue is largely a public policy question, not an exclusively scientific one."

The researchers hope to conduct future research investigating how differences between types of entertainment—violent video games, violent TV programs and films—influence desensitization to real violence. They also hope to investigate who is most likely to become desensitized as a result of exposure to violent video games.

"Several features of violent video games suggest that they may have even more pronounced effects on users than violent TV programs and films," said Carnagey.

> *"Playing violent video games probably
> will not turn your child into a
> psychopathic killer," [...] but I would
> want to know how the child treats
> his or her parents, how they treat
> their siblings, how much compassion
> they have."*

Violent Video Games Can Desensitize Young People

Shankar Vedantam

In the following viewpoint, Shankar Vedantam compares the interpretation by two different psychologists of the research that has been done on the effects of violent video games. While both psychologists view the results in different ways, Vedantam asserts, they each believe that the gaming does have some effect on behavior. One believes that it desensitizes young people to violence; the other believes the effects are more trivial and transient. Vedantam is a social science correspondent for NPR.

As you read, consider the following questions:

1. Why did the Supreme Court overturn a California ban on violent video games?
2. How and with whom are most experiments into the effects of violent video games conducted?
3. What two things does Ferguson believe are being mixed up in the assessment of the studies about violence and video games and what is his conclusion?

Scientists have long clashed over whether violent video games have an adverse effect on young people. Indeed, the conclusions of different groups of researchers are so contradictory they could give a tennis umpire whiplash.

The Supreme Court recently overturned a California ban on violent video games. The court said that video games, even offensive ones, were protected by the First Amendment, and that there wasn't clear evidence that playing games such as *Grand Theft Auto* and *Postal* really harmed people.

So what explains the vehement disagreements among scientists about the effects of these games? The irony is that scientists who think the games are harmful and those who think they're not are both looking at the same evidence. They just see two different things.

Most experiments into the effects of violent video games are done with college students. Researchers divide them into two groups. One group plays a violent game, the other a non-violent video game. Then researchers measure how students in each group feel and how they behave. You can't give young people guns and knives to see whether they'll kill each other after playing a violent video game, so scientists have come up with other ways to measure emotional responses.

Social psychologist Brad Bushman at Ohio State University once showed students violent pictures: one of a man shoving a gun down another man's throat; another of a man holding a knife to a woman's throat.

"What we found is for people who were exposed to a lot of violent video games, their brains did not respond to the violent images," Bushman said. "They were numb, if you will."

Bushman also had the students blast each other with loud noises.

"We try to make the noise as unpleasant as possible by thinking of every noise you hate," Bushman said. "So like fingernails scratching on a chalkboard, dentist drills, sirens."

Students could make the sound as loud as a smoke alarm, if they wanted. Some students in the experiments got really mean.

"Everybody was more aggressive if they'd played a violent game than if they'd played a nonviolent game, and the more numb they were, the more aggressive they were in terms of blasting their opponent with loud noise through headphones," Bushman said.

Desensitization Toward Violence?

That sounds airtight. Bushman believes that violent video games desensitize young people. Compared to people in the real world who are gentle and compassionate, students playing these games seem to be mean and hurtful.

But Chris Ferguson, a psychologist at the Texas A&M International University, disagrees. He's conducted similar experiments and also sees similar behavior changes among students. But he interprets them very differently.

Compared to people in the real world who shoot and stab one another, Ferguson said the changes in behavior he's seen among students are transient and trivial.

"You know most of the debate now is really on to these minor acts of aggressiveness," he said. "You know we're talking about little children sticking their tongues out at each other and that sort of thing."

Ferguson says it's easy to think senseless video game violence can lead to senseless violence in the real world. But he says that's mixing up two separate things.

"Many of the games do have morally objectionable material and I think that is where a lot of the debate on this issue went off

A NUMBING EFFECT

While violent video games may be creating aggressive tendencies in our youth, they are also desensitizing our adolescence from real-life violence. [...] the authors of the *Journal of Experimental Social Psychology* [...] performed a very interesting and effective study of desensitization of college students who played video games versus students who did not. After the researchers took baseline physiological measurements on heart rate and galvanic skin response, they allowed half of the 257 participants to play a violent video game, such as *Duke Nukem*, for 20 minutes, while the other half played a non-violent video game, such as *Pinball*. After the participants were pulled from their flashing TV screens, they were subjected to a series of real-life violent videos, while their physiological measurements were being taken again. The results were shocking. They found that the players who experienced the violent video games had, on average, a 15% lower heart rate than those who played a non-violent video game. Also, the ones exposed to the violent video games had a significantly lower perspiration rate during the video, as compared to those that did not partake in the shoot-em-up action.

[...] This means people who experience violent video games for a mere 20 minutes habituate or 'get used to' all the violence and eventually become physiologically numb to it.

"The Detrimental Effects of Violent Video Games on Society," Duckinator617, Teen Ink, October 15, 2016.

the rails," he said. "We kind of mistook our moral concerns about some of these video games, which are very valid—I find many of the games to be morally objectionable—and then assumed that what is morally objectionable is harmful."

In other words, if you define harm as getting in trouble with the police, violent video games probably aren't a risk. But if you're worried about lesser kinds of harm, they can be a risk.

"Playing violent video games probably will not turn your child into a psychopathic killer," Bushman said, "but I would want to know how the child treats his or her parents, how they treat their siblings, how much compassion they have."

So the dueling scientific studies aren't really at odds with each other—they just make different assumptions. Which may be why Bushman and Ferguson agree on one thing: as fathers, they've banned their own kids from playing violent video games.

"Granted, consuming countless hours of unfettered blood and gore can't be healthy. [...] But let's agree on this point: although it's tempting to assume that violence in video games translates to the real world, there is simply not enough evidence to support it."

Cooperative Video Gaming Can Increase Prosocial Behavior

Jeffrey MacCormack

In the following viewpoint, Jeffrey MacCormack contends that while playing violent video games may result in aggression, it is temporary and does not transfer to a player's personality. Violence is not the cause of aggression, but rather other factors are, such as the type of game, which device is used, and social aspects like competition and cooperation. The author argues that cooperative play increases prosocial behavior and aggression is mitigated when violence is part of a prosocial context, such as saving a loved one from danger. MacCormack is an assistant professor of educational psychology and inclusion at Queen's University, Canada.

"The Effects of Violent Video Games: Blasting the Myth," by Jeffrey MacCormack, The Artiface, June 14, 2015.

As you read, consider the following questions:

1. What are the two main messages from the research on violent video games?
2. What are the benefits of video game play?
3. What are the effects on behavior of cooperative game play?

In defence of his client Lee Boyd Malvo, one of the snipers who terrorized the greater Washington area during October of 2002, attorney Craig Cooley said that his client's mind state was altered by extended playing of violent video games (VVG). While this defence was not enough to keep Malvo from being convicted of the charges laid against him in a court of law, the relationship between antisocial behaviour and VVG appears to be quite strong in the court of public opinion. From the nightly news desk to the United States Senate (Anderson & Bushman, 2001), the message is clear: society needs to know the full effects of VVG.

With sales total of $800 million in the first 24 hours of sale of its most recent title, the *Grand Theft Auto* video game series is one of the most profitable titles of all time. Also famous for its violence, it remains one of the only games where a player can solicit the services of a prostitute and then stomp her to death to get back the money. Due to its popularity and the level of violence, the game is often the focus of attention during these debates (e.g. Kutner & Olson, 2008). The public wants to know what effect playing VVGs like *Grand Theft Auto 5* will have.

Here is the critical question: if a youth murders a woman in a virtual world, does that action have any relationship to actions, thoughts, or behaviours in the real-world? The National Rifle Association (widely known as NRA) has an answer for us. After a gunman killed 26 in an elementary school shooting in 2012, top lobbyist for the NRA, Wayne LaPierre, pointed to the video game industry to explain the violence. LaPierre called the video game industry a "shadow industry" that "sows violence against its own people," singling out *Bulletstorm*, *Grand Theft Auto*, *Mortal Kombat*, and *Splatterhouse*. Does LaPierre's explanation make sense? Do video games make killers?

Considering that 97% of adolescents play video games (Blumberg, Altschuler, Almonte, & Mileaf, 2013) for an average of seven hours a week (Janssen, Boyce & Pickett, 2012; some estimates are as high as 13 hours, see Adachi & Willoughby, 2011) and those who engage in extended video game play are more likely to prefer violent video games (Anderson & Bushman, 2001), empirically determining the impact of VVGs like *Grand Theft Auto* has never been more important.

What do we know about the effects of violent video games? Broadly speaking, we have two main messages from the research on VVG. The first message, that VVG play can improve performance of cognition tasks (e.g. visuo-spatial competences; e.g. Boot, Kramer, Simons, Fabiani, & Gratton, 2008), is widely accepted. The second message, that VVG play prompts aggression (e.g. Anderson & Bushman, 2001; Sherry, 2001), is hotly contested and generally misunderstood.

Benefits of VVG Play

As mentioned, the benefits of video game play are uncontroversial. It is widely believed that the inherent characteristics of the video game can improve learner motivation (MacCormack, 2013), allow active participation rather than passive reception (Buckley & Anderson, 2006), and promote development of skills through repeated practice (Anderson & Dill, 2000). Learning games can be designed to specifically teach isolated skills or foster broad outcomes like problem-solving.

A video game designed by cognitive psychologists called *Space Fortress* was shown to improve competences in novel tasks such as piloting skills (Gopher, Weil, & Bareket, 1994) and measures of physics knowledge (Frederiksen & White, 1989). A wealth of findings from clinical studies consistently shows that expert VVG players outperform those who do not play VVGs on spatial and perception tasks (Boot et al., 2008). For example, the shot accuracy of expert VVG players is so much higher than those who don't play VVGs, military training programs include components of video game training in real-world training (e.g. Israeli air force, Gopher, Weil, & Bareket, 1994; United States Marines, Buckley & Anderson, 2006).

Aggression and VVG Play

This leaves the question: do we have evidence that VVG play can cause aggression? Here's the quick answer: well, yes and no. Players of VVG display short-term aggression, a phenomenon known as "violent video game effect" (Sestir & Batholow, 2010). These effects don't last long and don't seem to change the personality of choices of the players. Aggressive feelings and thoughts last less than four minutes; aggressive behaviour and increased heart rate last until nine minutes (Barlett, Branch, Rodeheffer, & Harris, 2009).

Carnagey and Anderson (2005) designed a study to look specifically at how violence is treated in the game. The participants played a violent racing game called *Carmageddon 2*. In the game, the player races to a finish line while attacking other racers with weapons. The participants played in three modes which handled violence differently. For the first mode, violence was rewarded; in the second mode, violence was punished; and in the final mode, violence was absent. Carnagey and Anderson found that when violence is rewarded, aggressive emotion, thinking, and behaviour increases. When violence is punished, aggressive emotion is increased, but aggressive thinking and behavior were not increased (Carnagey & Anderson, 2005)

While the phenomenon of short-term violent video game effect has been held as truth since the 1980s when studies focused on participation at arcades (when at-home consoles were rare), studies conducted in the last few years have started to look at game features other than violence as the primary cause of aggression.

New generations of video games are much more sophisticated than previous generations. Whereas early study designs had a very short list of games title to choose from, modern games can choose games that best represent the exact recipes required (e.g. high competition, low violence; high frustration, low violence; high cooperation, high violence). The extended range of game types has allowed studies to control for features to determine their exact inter-relationship. Currently, researchers are focusing on three features as the most important components to explain aggression in video games: (i) competition; (ii) hardware; and (iii) social features.

Competition

Although there are exceptions to the rule, violence and competition are usually packaged together in video games. Most of the games listed as violent are also highly competitive so it has been difficult to see if violence or competition is the most salient component (Adachi & Willoughby, 2013). To remedy this flaw, researchers have been designing studies to specifically look at the role that competition plays in aggression. Aggressive behaviour is predicted by competition in video games irrespective of the games' violence (Adachi & Willoughby, 2013).

In one study, Schmierbach (2010) used three game modes of the same video game *HALO*. In the first game mode, the single player played against computer-controlled alien enemies (solo). In the second game mode, the player worked with other human players against alien enemies (cooperation). In the final mode, the player played against other human players (competition). Schmierbach found that playing competitively against other humans caused the most aggression and playing cooperatively with humans caused the least aggression. These findings align with other studies that have shown that competitive play modes were better predictors of aggressive behaviour than cooperative or solo modes (Adachi & Willoughby, 2011; Schmierbach, Xu, Oeldorf-Hirsch, & Dardis, 2012).

Hardware

The findings of research on the effect of the hardware have been mixed. Whether the player has a controller in hand or a model of a gun affects the level of aggression. The use of the light gun increased aggression levels (Barlett, Harris, & Baldassaro, 2007) which is consistent with research on effect of visual representation of weapons in priming for aggression "weapon effect" (Börsche, 2010). Some studies have found that the more realistic the depiction of violence, the more aggression is created. In that way, the development of technology creates a deeper emersion into increasingly realistic virtual environments and is a proxy of level of aggressive cognition (Sherry, 2001). Other studies have found the opposite: that the quality of the depiction of the video game (e.g. graphics capacity of the console) does not mediate the aggressive response to violent video games (Barlett, Rodeheffer, Baldassaro, Hinkin, & Harris, 2008).

The next step in technology will likely be the mainstream use of immersive virtual environment platforms. The displays of immersive virtual environment platforms are not through a screen like typical game experiences. Immersive virtual environment screens are head-mounted displays that track head movement and body actions. Use of immersive virtual environments for violent games increased aggression compared to violent games using screen-based outputs (Persky & Blascovich, 2007).

Social Features

Despite the stereotype of a lonely youth playing video games in the basement of his parents' home, video games are a social activity. Web interfaces like Twitch.tv provide platforms for gamers to share content and communicate. This new level of game-related socialization demonstrate that gaming is not a solitary activity. Unfortunately, there has not been much attention paid to the social benefits of membership in gaming communities in the research. Moving forward, social researchers will know more about online interactions and how gamers co-exist in these communities.

Furthermore, studies show that enjoyment is significantly improved by cooperative play with another human regardless of relational ties (Schmierback et al., 2012). In game behaviour can be a factor in whether the overall effect is positive or negative; for example, coordination in role-playing games increases prosocial behavior (De Simone, 2013). Cooperative play of video games with no other prosocial content increases prosocial behavior (Sestir & Batholow, 2010) Video games with prosocial content increased prosocial behavior (Greitemeyer & Osswald, 2010). Aggressive outcomes are mitigated when violence in video games is a part of a prosocial context (e.g. protecting a loved one from danger; Gitter Ewell, Guadagno, Stillman, & Baumeister, 2013).

NOTE: if you're interested in knowing more about how behaviour is rated as aggressive or prosocial, you may want to know how it is measured in the lab. Commonly used aggression measures fit broadly into two categories: ambiguous and unambiguous measurements. An example of an ambiguous measurement is a lexical test. The participant is asked to complete a word with letters missing (e.g. "K I _ _"). Participants who have recently played VVGs are more likely to respond with words like "kick" or "kill" than words like "kiss" or "kiln" (Bösche, 2010). An example of an unambiguous measurement is the Hot Sauce Paradigm. The participant is asked to season a plate of food for another person who does not like spicy food using one of four hot sauce varieties. Participants who have recently played VVGs are more likely to season the plate of food with the spiciest sauce.

Ask your grandmother what happens to kids who play violent video games and you may be told that *Call of Duty Black Ops 3* changes docile adolescents into rage-hounds. It's not just your grandmother; perhaps we all believe that a little bit. The problem is that it is not true. While violent video games may cause aggression, the "violent video game effect" is temporary and does not transfer to personality. Furthermore, the culprit in VVG is not the violence. People become agitated because of game types, devices, and the social aspects of video games. Think of the last time you rage-quit

HALO. Was it because the inherent violence of the narrative finally wore you down? Or was it that a 13-year old from Wisconsin noob-tubed you while shouting homophobic insults?

Granted, consuming countless hours of unfettered blood and gore can't be healthy. Of course, no one is recommending you decorate your 5-year old's birthday party with a *Witcher 3* theme. But let's agree on this point: although it's tempting to assume that violence in video games translates to the real world, there is simply not enough evidence to support it.

Works Cited

Adachi, P. & Willoughby, T. (2011). The effect of video game competition and violence on aggressive behavior: Which characteristic has the greatest influence? Psychology of Violence, 1, 259-274.

Anderson, C. & Bushman, B. (2001). Effects of violent video games on aggression behavior, aggressive cognition, aggressive affect, physiological arousal, and prosocial behavior: A meta-analytic review of the scientific literature. Psychological Science,12, 353-359.

Anderson, C. & Dill, K. (2000). Video games and aggressive thoughts, feelings, and behavior in the laboratory and in life. Journal of Personality and Social Psychology, 78, 772-790.

Barlett, C., Branch, O., Rodeheffer, C. & Harris, R. (2009). How long do the short-term violent video game effects last? Aggressive Behavior, 35, 225-236.

Barlett, C., Harris, R. & Baldassaro, R. (2007). Longer you play, the more hostile you feel: Examination of first person shooter video games and aggression during video game play. Aggressive Behavior, 33, 486-497.

Barlett, C., Rodeheffer, C., Baldassaro, R., Hinkin, M. & Harris, R. (2008). The effect of advances in video game technology and content on aggressive cognitions, hostility, and heart rate. Media Psychology, 11, 540-565.

Blumberg, F., Altshuler, E., Almonte, D. & Mileaf, M. (2013). The impact of recreational video game play on children's and adolescents' congition. In F. C. Blumberg & S.M. Fisch (Eds.), Digital Games: A Context for Cognitive Development. New Directions for Child and Adolescent Development, 139, 41-50.

Boot, W., Kramer, A., Simons, D. Fabiani, M. & Gratton, G. (2008). The effects of video game playing on attention, memory, and executive control. Acta Psychologia, 129, 387-398.

Bösche, W. (2010). Violent video games prime both aggressive and positive cognitions. Journal of Media Psychology, 22, 139-146.

Buckley, K. & Anderson, C. (2006). A theoretical model of the effects and consequences of playing video games. In P.Vorderer & J. Bryant (Eds.), Playing video games—Motive, responses, and consequences (pp. 363–378). Mahwah, NJ:LEA.

Carnagey, M. & Anderson, C. (2005). The effects of reward and punishment in violent video games on aggressive affect, cognition, and behavior. Psychological Science, 16, 882-889.

De Simone, J. (2013). What is good can also be bad: The prosocial and antisocial in-game behaviors of young video game players. Atlantic Journal of Communication, 21, 149-163.

Frederiksen, J. & White, B. (1989). An approach to training based upon principled task decomposition. Acta Psychologica , 71, 89-146.

Gitter, S., Ewell, P., Guadagno, R., Stillman, R. & Baumeister, R. (2013). Virtually justifiable homicide: The effects of prosocial contexts on the link between violent video games, aggression, and prosocial and hostile cognition. Aggressive Behavior, 39, 346-354.

Gopher, D., Weil, M., & Bareket, T. (1994). Transfer of skill from a computer game trainer to flight. Human Factors, 36, 387-405.

Greitemeyer, T.& Osswald, S. (2010). Effects of prosocial video games on prosocial behavior. Journal of Personality and Social Personality, 98, 211-221.

Kutner, L. & Olson, C. (2008, April 8). Violence and video games. Toronto Star. p.1. Retrieved from http://www.thestar.com/life/parent/2008/04/28/violence_and_video_games.html.

MacCormack, J. (2013, Fall). Toys as tools: Using e-games for learning, ETFO Voice, Retrieved from: http://etfovoice.ca/toys-as-tools-using-e-games-for-learning.

Persky, S. & Blascovich, J. (2007). Immersive virtual environments versus traditional platforms: Effects of violent and nonviolent video game play. Media Psychology, 10, 135-156.

Schmierbach, M. (2010). "Killing spree": Exploring the connection between competitive game play and aggressive cognition. Communication Research, 37, 256-274.

Schmierbach, M., Xu, Q., Oeldorf-Hirsch, A. & Dardis, F. (2012). Electronic friend or virtual foe: Exploring the role of competitive and cooperative multiplayer video game modes in fostering enjoyment. Media Psychology, 15, 356-371.

Sestir, M. & Batholow, B. (2010). Violent and nonviolent video games produce opposing effects on aggressive and prosocial outcomes. Journal of Experimental Social Psychology, 46, 934-942.

Sherry, J. (2001). The effects of violent video games on aggression: A meta-analysis. Human Communication Research, 27, 409-431.

> "*Thus, violent games may increase aggression in part by stressing players out. Although nobody actually gets killed in a violent game, players do experience increased stress, which makes them more cranky and prone to aggress against others.*"

Playing Violent Video Games Increases Stress

Youssef Hasan, Laurent Begue, and Brad J. Bushman

In the following viewpoint, Youssef Hasan, Laurent Begue, and Brad J. Bushman examine stress as the possible instrument that results in aggressive behavior after playing violent video games. Cardiac coherence, the synchronization of the rhythm of breathing to the rhythm of the heart, was used as a measuring device in this study. Increased stress causes larger fluctuations in heart rate variability, resulting in a decrease in cardiac coherence. As predicted, it went down after participants played violent video games, indicating a possible reason why violent games result in aggression: aggression is induced by stress. Hasan is an assistant professor at Qatar University. Begue is professor of social psychology at the University of Grenoble Alpes. Bushman is Professor of Communication and Psychology, The Ohio State University.

"Violent Video Games Stress People Out and Make Them More Aggressive," by Youssef Hasan, Laurent Begue, and Brad J. Bushman, John Wiley & Sons, Inc., October 24, 2012. Reprinted by permission.

As you read, consider the following questions:

1. What was the main purpose of this study?
2. How does cardiac coherence measure stress?
3. What were three limitations of this study?

Introduction

> "Stress is an ignorant state. It believes that everything is
> an emergency."
>
> —Natalie Golberg, American author

In emergency situations, the body responds with stress. Stress is an undesirable state because it can have harmful effects on the body, such as cardiovascular disease (Weiten, Dunn, & Hammer, 2011). Most people already experience enough stress in their lives without intentionally exposing themselves to more stress. We argue that violent video game players do just that—they intentionally expose players to stressful situations in which enemies are trying to kill them. Although some video games can have a relaxing effect on players (Russoniello, O'Brien, & Parks, 2009; Whitaker & Bushman, 2012), violent video games have the opposite effect. Research has shown that violent video games increases physiological arousal, such as heart rate (Barlett & Rodeheffer, 2009), blood pressure and skin conductance (Arriaga, Esteves, Carneiro, & Monteiro, 2006), and stress hormones such as epinephrine and nor-epinephrine (Lynch, 1999). Although nobody actually dies, violent players may still experience stress.

It is well known that violent video games increase aggression (see Anderson et al., 2010 for a metaanalytic review). It is also well known that that stressful situations such as crowding, unpredictable noise, unpleasant odors, and hot temperatures increase aggression (see Bushman & Huesmann, 2010 for a review). The present research links these two well-established empirical findings by investigating increased stress as one possible explanation of why violent video games increase aggression. Rather than relying on self-report measures of stress that may be subject to demand characteristics and other biases (e.g., Nisbett & Wilson, 1977), we examine for the first time cardiac coherence as a possible mediator of the link between exposure to violent video games and subsequent aggression. We chose to focus on cardiac coherence because it is an excellent measure of reduced stress.

Cardiac Coherence

Heart rate is affected by the autonomic nervous system (Acharya, Joseph, Kannathal, Lim, & Suri, 2006; Fraser & Swinney, 1986; Kleiger et al., 1991). The autonomic nervous system is divided into two opposing subsystems: the sympathetic nervous system and the parasympathetic nervous system. The sympathetic nervous system works like an accelerator on the heart—it increases heart rate to mobilize the body in response to stress, called a fight–flight response. In contrast, the parasympathetic nervous system works like a brake on the heart—it promotes maintenance of the body at rest by controlling most of the body's internal organs. Imbalance in the autonomic nervous system occurs when people experience negative emotions (Childre & Cryer, 2004).

Breathing influences the way the autonomic nervous system regulates heart rate. Inhalation inhibits the parasympathetic system and increases heart rate, whereas exhalation stimulates the parasympathetic system and decreases heart rate. This rhythmic shift in heart rate associated with respiration is known as respiratory sinus arrhythmia (Berntson, Casioppo, & Quigley, 1993; Chess, Tam, & Calaresu, 1975).

Heart rate variability is the amount heart rate fluctuates, as measured by the variation in the beat-tobeat interval. Heart rate variability is an indicator of greater autonomic nervous system balance (Lehrer, Woolfolk, & Sime, 2007), and reflects the influence of the autonomic nervous system on how hard the heart works (Milicevi ˘ c, 2005). Heart rate variability was first used clinically in 1965 when doctors noted that fetal distress was preceded by changes in interbeat intervals before any appreciable change occurred in the heart rate itself (Hon & Lee, 1965).

Directly relevant to the present study is a large body of research showing a link between lower heart rate variability and negative emotions such as anger (Acharya et al., 2006; Carney & Rich, 1988; Fraser & Swinney, 1986; Kleiger et al., 1991; McCraty, Atkinson, Tiller, Rein, & Watkins, 1995; Milicevi ˘ c, 2005). Research also shows a link between lower rate variability and antisocial behavior, such as aggression (Lahey, Hart, Pliszka, Applegate, &McBurnett, 1993; Scarpa & Haden, 2006; Scarpa, Tanaka, & Haden, 2008; Susman & Pajer, 2004). Likewise, reduced respiratory sinus arrhythmia is linked to antisocial behavior (Mezzacappa et al., 1997). Although previous research has linked exposure to violence to increased heart rate and faster respiration (Fourie, 2008), the link between exposure to violence and lower heart rate variability remains unclear. Generally, there are no gender differences in heart rate variability (Acton, 2011; Ramaekers, Ector, Aubert, Rubens, & Van de Werf, 1998).

Research has shown that breathing can increase heart rate variability and respiratory sinus arrhythmia, resulting in a balance of sympathetic and parasympathetic activity that reduces stress and provides greater relaxation and feelings of well being (Bolis, Licinio, & Govoni, 2002). Cardiac coherence is defined as the synchronization of the rhythm of breathing to the rhythm of the heart (Carney & Rich, 1988; McCraty et al., 1995). It is reflected by a sine wave-like pattern in the heart rhythms consisting of a smooth repetitive oscillation. One component of this pattern is frequency, which determines how many oscillations occur within a unit time interval. At a frequency of about 0.1 hertz, the oscillation in heart rate between exhalation and inhalation tends to be maximal (Vaschillo, Lehrer, Rishe, & Konstantinov, 2002). This usually occurs at about six breaths per minute. Cardiac coherence is a state in which heart rate variability is highly regular (Church, 2007). Although heart rate variability is defined as beat-to-beat changes in heart rate, cardiac coherence is defined as the smoothness or synchronization of these changes as they are influenced by the automatic nervous system (Childre & Cryer, 2004).

Cardiac coherence is a relatively new measure of autonomic nervous system balance (Tiller, McCraty, & Atkinson, 1996). When cardiac coherence occurs, the frontal, temporal, and parietal-occipital regions of the brain are activated; the autonomic nervous system is balanced; and the body functions with increased harmony and efficiency (Carney & Rich, 1988; Childre & Cryer, 2004; McCraty et al., 1995), such as in the circulatory and nervous systems (McCraty & Tomasino, 2006).

Previous research has shown when people experience positive emotions such as appreciation, joy, gratitude, and love, fluctuations in heart rate variability are small and cardiac coherence occurs (Childre & Cryer, 2004; Church, 2007). Previous research has shown that cardiac coherence is associated with decreased anxiety and depression, decreased physical symptoms related to stress, increased immune functions, decreased cortisol production (a stress hormone), and increased DHEA (Dehydroepiandrosterone) define as the antistress hormone that keeps in check and corrects blood cortisol levels (Mikulka, 2011; Wickens, 2009). Biofeedback programs designed to reduce stress often use breathing and relaxation techniques to achieve a state of cardiac coherence (Maria, 2009; Nunan et al., 2009). In contrast, when people experience negative emotions such as stress, anger, frustration, sadness, and anxiety, fluctuations in heart rate variability are large and cardiac coherence decreases (Childre & Cryer, 2004; Church, 2007;), a state called cardiac incoherence. When people feel negative emotions, cardiac incoherence signals the brain, impedes thinking, and hinders decision-making (Feinstein, 2006).

Cardiac coherence also has at least six other attributes that are desirable to researchers studying video game effects. First, cardiac coherence is more directly related to negative affect such as stress than other physiological measures (Childre & Cryer, 2004; McCraty & Tomasino, 2006) because it can distinguish sympathetic from parasympathetic regulation of the heart rate (Tiller et al., 1996).

Second, cardiac coherence is less invasive than other physiological measures such as skin conductance, blood pressure, and heart rate (e.g., it is difficult to play a video game with finger clips or arm cuffs). Cardiac coherence is measured using a comfortable clip that attaches to the earlobe. Measures of heart rate, blood pressure, and skin conductance use pressurized cuffs or sensors on either the upper arm or the finger. These often draw attention and can even be painful (especially the blood pressure cuff), which can elicit emotional reactions (Kahneman, Diener, & Schwarz, 2003). Third, cardiac coherence is generally stable against various forms of environmental disturbance, such as muscle movements that often occur when playing video games. Fourth, cardiac coherence is less subject to demand characteristics than self-report measures of stress. Fifth, cardiac coherence equipment is relatively inexpensive in comparison to other physiological equipment. Sixth, cardiac coherence measures are very easy for researchers to use.

Present Research

In the present study, participants were randomly assigned to play either a violent or nonviolent video game while their cardiac coherence was measured. Next, they competed against an ostensible partner on a task in which the winner could blast the loser with loud noise through headphones. The intensity and duration of noise participants gave their ostensible partner was used to measure aggressive behavior. We predicted that participants who played a violent game would have lower cardiac coherence than participants who played a nonviolent game, and that cardiac coherence, in turn, would be negatively related to aggression.

Method

Participants
Participants were 77 French university students (83% female; Mage = 20.1, SD = 3.1; 100% Caucasian) who received course credit. Aggr. Behav.

Procedure

Participants were told that the researchers were studying the effects of the brightness of video games on visual perception and physiological arousal. They were asked if they had any vision problems or cardiovascular disease; none did. After informed consent was obtained, a 1-min baseline measure of cardiac coherence was obtained using a Stress Pilot biofeedback device (Biocomfort Diagnostics, Wendlingen, Germany), a soft, comfortable clip that attaches to the left earlobe. Because the impact of breathing on heart rate variability is greatest at six breaths a minute (Gevirtz & Lehrer, 2003), the Stress Pilot device measures heart rate variability and respiration rate at a rate of six breaths. Participants were not instructed to engage in paced breathing. The device randomly selects six breaths from the breathing cycle, and then measures heart rate variability and respiration rate at a rate of these six breaths. The Stress Pilot device calculates the maximum and minimum heart rate for each breath, and then calculates the quotient of the maximum to minimum heart rate for this breath. Compared with statistical parameters (e.g., the standard deviation), this quotient is less affected by artifacts such as body movements.

Next, participants were then randomly assigned to play a violent or nonviolent game for 20 min while cardiac coherence was recorded. To increase the generalizability of findings (Wells & Windschitl, 1999), we used three violent games (*Condemned 2*, *Call of Duty 4*, and *The Club*; all rated 18+, for players at least 18-years-old) and three nonviolent games (*S3K Superbike*, *Dirt 2* and *Pure*; all rated 10+, for players at least 10-years-old). Before they played the game, participants were given instructions on how to play. After playing the game, participants rated how absorbing, action packed, arousing, boring, difficult, enjoyable, entertaining, exciting, frustrating, fun, involving, stimulating, and violent it was (1 = not at all to 7 = extremely). The violent rating was used as a manipulation check. The other ratings were used as possible covariates to control for differences between video games besides violent content. Participants also listed their three favorite games.

To control for habitual exposure to violent video games, we counted the number of games rated 18+ for violent content (0, 1, 2, or 3 games), as in our previous research (Hasan, Begue, & ` Bushman, 2012; Whitaker & Bushman, 2012). However, because the same pattern of results was obtained with and without the covariates, we used the simpler analyses that excluded the covariates.

Next, participants completed a 25-trial competitive reaction time task with an ostensible partner of the same sex in which the winner could blast the loser with loud noise through headphones. The noise levels ranged from Level 1 = 60 decibels to Level 10 = 105 decibels (about the same level as a fire alarm). A nonaggressive no-noise option (Level 0) was also provided. The winner could also determine the duration of the loser's suffering by controlling the noise duration (Level 1 = 0.5 sec to Level 10 = 5 sec). The participant won 12 of the 25 trials (randomly determined). The ostensible partner set random noise intensities and durations across the 25 trials. Basically, within the ethical limits of the laboratory, participants controlled a weapon that could be used to blast their partner with unpleasant noise. This is a well-validated measure of laboratory aggression (e.g., Giancola & Zeichner, 1995) that has been used for decades (Taylor, 1967). Finally, participants were probed for suspicion and debriefed. None of the participants expressed suspicion about the study.

Results

Preliminary Analyses
Gender differences. There were no significant effects involving gender on either cardiac coherence or aggression, so the data from men and women were combined.

Exemplars of violent and nonviolent video games. No significant differences were found among the three different violent games or among the three different nonviolent games on either cardiac coherence or aggression (Ps > .05). Thus, the three violent games were combined and the three nonviolent games were combined for subsequent analyses.

Manipulation check of violent content of video games. As expected, violent video games were rated as more violent (M = 5.85, SD = 1.44) than were nonviolent video games (M = 2.05, SD = 1.27), $F(1,76) = 149.45$, $P < .001$, d = 2.80. Thus, the violent game manipulation was successful.

Primary Analyses

Cardiac coherence. Cardiac coherence was analyzed using a 2 (violent vs. nonviolent video game) × 2 (baseline vs. during game play) mixed ANOVA, with the first factor between-subjects and the second factor within-subjects. As expected, there was a significant interaction between video game content and measurement time on cardiac coherence values, $F(1,74) = 19.87$, $P < .0001$. Participants who played a violent game had significantly lower cardiac coherence values than did participants who had played a nonviolent video game, $F(1,75) = 19.49$, $P < .0001$ d = 1.02. Cardiac coherence values at baseline did not differ for participants who played violent and nonviolent games, $F(1,75) = 0.53$, $P < .47$ d = 0.17, indicating that random assignment to conditions was effective.

Aggressive behavior. As expected, noise intensity and duration levels across the 25 trials were significantly correlated (r = .90 $P < .0001$), and were therefore averaged to form a more reliable measure of aggression. As expected, participants who played a violent game were more aggressive (M = 4.70, SD = 1.85) than were participants who played a nonviolent game (M = 3.76, SD = 1.46), $F(1,75) = 5.99$, $P < .05$, d = 0.59.

Mediation analysis. Finally, we tested whether cardiac coherence mediated the effect of playing a violent video game on aggressive behavior using bootstrap procedures (Preacher & Hayes, 2004). As can be seen in Figure 3, the indirect effect of violent video game exposure on aggression, through cardiac coherence, was significant (95% CI = −0.83 to −0.13, which excludes the value 0). When both video game content and cardiac coherence were both included in the model, the effect of video game content was nonsignificant (P > .24), whereas the effect of cardiac coherence was significant (P < .03).

Discussion

Consistent with many previous studies (see Anderson et al., 2010, for a meta-analytic review), participants who played a violent video game were significantly more aggressive afterwards than were participants who played a nonviolent video game. Violent game players gave their ostensible partners louder and longer noise blasts through headphones than did nonviolent game players.

The main purpose of the present research, however, was not to replicate previous findings showing that violent video games increase aggression. Our main purpose was to investigate cardiac coherence as a mediator of the link between exposure to violent video games and aggressive behavior. Our results showed that violent video games decreased cardiac coherence. Cardiac coherence, in turn, was negatively related to aggression.

These findings offer one possible reason why violent game players were more aggressive. Violent games stress people out, and stressed out people tend to be cranky and aggressive. These findings are consistent with the General Aggression Model (e.g., Anderson & Bushman, 2002) and with cognitive-neoassociation theory (e.g., Berkowitz, 1990), which both propose that aversive emotional states increase aggression.

Limitations and Future Research

The present study, like all studies, has limitations. Although we can make causal inferences on the effects of violent video games, we cannot make causal inferences on the effects of cardiac coherence on aggression (see Bullock, Green, & Ha, 2010). Unfortunately, it is not possible to directly manipulate cardiac coherence (Madanmohan, Prakash, & Bhavanani, 2005). One can only manipulate factors that are expected to in- fluence cardiac coherence, such as mood, breathing, and exercise. Second, we only measured one type of aggressive behavior (e.g., administering noise blasts to an opponent during a competitive game). Our findings may not generalize to more planned and thoughtful forms of aggression.

Another limitation is the large percentage of females in our study. Although we found no main or interactive effects involving gender, it is difficult to conclusively test for gender differences when the number of males and females is not equal.

Another limitation is that we did not include other physiological measures such as blood pressure, heart rate, and skin conductance. It would be interesting to see how cardiac coherence compares to other physiological measures that might also mediate the effect of violent video games on aggression. Nor did we measure other possible mediators such as aggressive cognition and hostile affect. In the General Aggression Model (Anderson & Bushman, 2002), these internal states are all interconnected. Thus, we do not know if cardiac coherence is a unique mediator of violent video game effects on aggression after controlling for other potential mediators. This remains an interesting topic for future research.

We did not measure self-reported stress because we were afraid that participants would become suspicious if we did. Thus, we can only infer based on previous research that cardiac coherence is linked to stress. However, numerous previous studies have shown that cardiac coherence is a well-accepted physiological measure of stress (e.g., Maria, 2009; Nunan et al., 2009).

Conclusions

As Natalie Golberg noted, "Stress is an ignorant state. It believes that everything is an emergency." Violent game players are placed in emergency situations in which many enemies are trying to kill them. One consequence of this exposure is an increase in stress. The present research showed that violent games reduced cardiac coherence. Cardiac coherence, in turn, was negatively associated with aggression. Thus, violent games may increase aggression in part by stressing players out. Although nobody actually gets killed in a violent game, players do experience increased stress, which makes them more cranky and prone to aggress against others.

References

Acharya, U. R., Joseph, P. K., Kannathal, N., Lim, C. M., & Suri, J. S. (2006). Heart rate variability: A review. Medical and Biological Engineering and Computing, 44, 1031–1051.

Acton, Q. A. (2011). Issues in neuropsychology, neuropsychiatry, and psychophysiology. Atlanta, GA: Scholarly Editions.

Anderson, C. A., & Bushman, B. J. (2002). Human aggression. Annual Review of Psychology, 53, 27–51.

Anderson, C. A., Shibuya, A., Ihori, N., Swing, E. L., Bushman, B. J., Sakamoto, A., . . . , C. P. (2010). Violent video game effects on aggression, empathy, and prosocial behavior in Eastern and Western countries: A meta-analytic review. Psychological Bulletin, 136, 151–173.

Arriaga, P., Esteves, F., Carneiro, P., & Monteiro, M. B. (2006). Violent computer games and their effects on state hostility and physiological arousal. Aggressive Behavior, 32, 146–158.

Barlett, C. P., & Rodeheffer, C. (2009). Effects of realism on extended violent and nonviolent video game play on aggressive thoughts, feelings, and physiological arousal. Aggressive Behavior, 35, 213–224.

Berkowitz, L. (1990). On the formation and regulation of anger and aggression: A cognitive-neoassociationistic analysis. American Psychologist, 45, 494–403.

Berntson, G. G., Casioppo, J. T., & Quigley, K. S. (1993). Cardiac psychophysiology and autonomic space in humans: Emirical prespective and conceptual implications. Psychological Bulletin, 114, 296–322.

Bolis, L., Licinio, J., & Govoni, S. (2002). Handbook of the autonomic nervous system in health and disease. New York: Marcel Dekker.

Bullock, J. G., Green, D. P., & Ha, S. E. (2010). Yes, but what's the mechanism? (Don't expect an easy answer). Journal of Personality and Social Psychology, 98, 550–558.

Bushman, B. J., & Huesmann, L. R. (2010). Aggression. In: S. T. Fiske, D. T. Gilbert, & G. Lindzey (Eds.), In Handbook of social psychology (pp. 833–863, 5th edn, Ch. 23). New York: John Wiley & Sons.

Carney, R. M., & Rich, M. W. (1988). The relationship between heart rate and heart rate variability and depression in patients with coronary artery disease. Journal of Psychosomatic Research, 32, 159–164.

Chess, G. F., Tam, R. M. K., & Calaresu, F. R. (1975). Influence of cardiac neural inputs on rhythmic variations of heart period in the cat. American Physiological Society, 228, 775–780.

Childre, D. L., & Cryer, B. (2004). From chaos to coherence: The power to change performance. Boston, MA: Heartmath.

Church, D. (2007). The genie in your genes: Epigenetic medicine and the new biology of intention. Santa Rosa: Energy Psychology Press.

Feinstein, S. (2006). The Praeger handbook of learning and the brain. Westport, CT: Praeger.

Fourie, P. J. (2008). Media studies policy management and media representation. Cape Town: Juta.

Fraser, A. M., & Swinney, H. L. (1986). Independent coordinates for strange attractors from mutual information. Physical Review A, 33, 1134–1140.

Gevirtz, R. N., & Lehrer, P. (2003). Resonant frequency heart rate biofeedback. In: M. Schwartz & F. Andrasik (Eds.), Biofeedback: A practitioner's guide (3rd edn., pp. 245–250). New York: The Guildford Press.

Giancola, P. R., & Zeichner, A. (1995). Construct validity of a competitive reaction- time aggression paradigm. Aggressive Behavior, 21, 199–204.

Hasan, Y., Begue, L., & Bushman, B. J. (2012). Viewing the world ` through "blood-red tinted glasses": The hostile expectation bias mediates the link between violent video game exposure and aggression. Journal of Experimental Social Psychology, 48, 953–956.

Hon, E. H., & Lee, S. T. (1965). Electronic evaluations of the fetal heart rate patterns preceding fetal death, further observations. American Journal of Obstetrics & Gynecology, 87, 814–26.

Kahneman, D., Diener, E., & Schwarz, N. (2003). Well-being: The foundations of hedonic psychology. New York: Russell Sage Foundation Publications. Aggr. Behav. Violent Video Games, Stress, & Aggression 7

Kleiger, R. E., Bigger, J. T., Bosner, M. S., Chung, M. K., Cook, J. R., Rolnitzky, L. M., . . . Fleiss, J. L. (1991). Stability over time of variables measuring heart rate variability in normal subjects. American Journal of Cardiology, 68, 626–630.

Lahey, B. B., Hart, E. L., Pliszka, S., Applegate, B., & McBurnett, K. (1993). Neurophysiological correlates of conduct disorder: A rationale and a review of research. Journal of Clinical Child Psychology, 22, 141–153.

Lehrer, P. M., Woolfolk, R. L., & Sime, W. E. (2007). Principles and practice of stress mangement. New York: Guilford.

Lynch, P. J. (1999). Hostility, type A behavior, and stress hormones at rest and after playing violent video games in teenagers. Psychosomatic Medicine, 56, 113–152. Madanmohan, M. D., Prakash, E. S., & Bhavanani, A. B. (2005). Correlation between short-term heart rate variability indices and heart rate blood pressure indices, pressor reactivity to isometric handgrip in healthy young male subjects. Indian Journal of Physiology and Pharmacology, 49, 132–138.

Maria, B. L. (2009). Current management in child neurology (4th ed.). Shelton: People's Medical Publishing House.

McCraty, R. (2002). Influence of cardiac afferent input on heart-brain synchronization and cognitive performance. International Journal of Psychophysiology, 45, 72–73.

McCraty, R., Atkinson, M., Tiller, W. A., Rein, G., & Watkins, A. D. (1995). The effects of emotions on short-term power spectral analysis of heart rate variability. American Journal of Cardiology, 76, 1089–1093.

McCraty, R., & Tomasino, D. (2006). Emotional stress, positive emotions, and psychophysiological coherence. In B. B. Arnetz & R. Ekman (Eds.), Stress in health and disease (pp. 342–365). Weinheim, Germany: Wiley-VCH.

Mezzacappa, E., Tremblay, R., Kindlon, D., Saul, J., Arseneault, L., Seguin, J., ... Earls, F. (1997). Anxiety, antisocial behavior, and heart rate regulation in adolescent males. Journal of Child Psychology and Psychiatry, 38, 457–469.

Mikulka, C. (2011). Peace in the heart and home: A down-to-earth guide for creating a better life. Woolwich Township, NJ: Kittacanoe press.

Milicevi ˇ c, G. (2005). Low to high frequency ratio of heart ´ rate variability spectra fails to describe sympatho-vagal balance in cardiac patients. Collegium Antropologicum, 29, 295– 300.

Nisbett, R., & Wilson, T. (1977). Telling more than we can know: Verbal reports on mental processes. Psychological Review, 84(3), 231–259.

Nunan, D., Donovan, G., Jakovljevic, D. G., Hodges, L. D., Sandercock, G. R., & Brodie, D. A. (2009). Validity and reliability of shortterm heart-rate variability from the Polar S810. Medicine and Science in Sports and Exercise, 41, 243–250.

Preacher, K. J., & Hayes, A. F. (2004). SPSS and SAS procedures for estimating indirect effects in simple mediation models. Behavior Research Methods, Instruments, & Computers, 36, 717–731.

Ramaekers, D., Ector, H., Aubert, A. E., Rubens, A., & Van deWerf, F. (1998). Heart rate variability and heart rate in healthy volunteers. Is the female autonomic nervous system cardioprotective? European Heart Journal, 19, 1334–1341.

Russoniello, C. V., O'Brien, K., & Parks, J. M. (2009). The effectiveness of casual video games in improving mood and decreasing stress. Journal of Cyber Therapy & Rehabilitation, 1, 53–66.

Scarpa, A., & Haden, S. C. (2006). Psychophysiological, behavioral, and emotional distinctions between childhood reactive and proactive aggression. Paper Presented at the XIX world meeting of the International Society for Research on Aggression, Minneapolis, Minnesota.

Scarpa, A., Tanaka, A., & Haden, S. C. (2008). Biosocial bases of reactive and proactive aggression: The roles of community violence exposure and heart rate. Journal of Community Psychology, 36 969– 988.

Susman, E. J., & Pajer, K. (2004). Biology behavior integration and antisocial behaavior in girls. InM. Putallaz & K. L. Bierman (Eds.), Aggression, antisocial behavior, and violence among girls (p. 23–47). New York: Guilford Press.

Taylor, S. P. (1967). Aggressive behavior and physiological arousal as a function of provocation and the tendency to inhibit aggression. Journal of Personality, 35, 297–310.

Tiller, W. A., McCraty, R., & Atkinson, M. (1996). Cardiac coherence: A new, noninvasive measure of autonomic nervous system order. Alternative Therapies in Health and Medicine, 2, 52–65.

Vaschillo, E., Lehrer, P., Rishe, N., & Konstantinov, M. (2002). Heart rate variability biofeedback as a method for assessing baroreflex function: A preliminary study of resonance in the cardiovascular system. Applied Psychophysiology and Biofeedback, 27, 1–27.

Weiten, W., Dunn, D. S., & Hammer, E. Y. (2011). Psychology applied to modern life: Adjustment in the 21st century. Belmont, CA: Wadsworth/Cengage.

Wells, G. L., & Windschitl, P. D. (1999). Stimulus sampling and social psychological experimentation. Personality and Social Psychology Bulletin, 25, 1115–1125.

Whitaker, J. L., & Bushman, B. J. (2012). "Remain calm. Be kind": Effects of relaxing video games on aggressive and prosocial behavior. Social Psychological and Personality Science, 3, 88–92.

Wickens, A. (2009). Introduction to Biopsychology. 3rd Edition. Harlow, UK: Pearson-Prentice Hall.

> "*There is a reason so many people
> turn to gaming, and if recent research
> is any indication, it's because video
> games provide a tremendous vehicle
> for stress relief in anyone's life, (plus,
> they're fun.)*"

Playing Video Games Reduces Stress

Ryan Dube

*In the following viewpoint, Ryan Dube makes the case that playing
violent video games does not increase stress, as others have argued.
In fact, playing these games actually can be used as a vehicle for de-
stressing and working out feelings of anger and depression. They are,
after all, games, which are meant to be fun. Dube cites several studies
to support his position that playing violent video games can have
a positive effect on mental health and recovery from work-related
stress. Dube is managing editor for MUO (MakeUseOf) magazine.*

As you read, consider the following questions:

1. What are the gamer demographics cited in this article?
2. What is a common answer to the question, "Why do you
   play video games?"
3. What was the final conclusion of the researchers,
   according to the author?

"Science Proves that Playing Video Games Reduces Your Stress," by Ryan Dube,
Makeuseof.com, September 11, 2015. Reprinted by permission.

Playing video games can relieve your stress, reduce your depression, and make you feel better.

That may sound like a big claim to make, but at this point there's plenty of evidence available to support it. Enough evidence in fact, that if video games aren't a regular part of your life right now, adding a bit of game-playing time to your schedule could actually improve your mental health in many surprising ways.

This topic is not without its controversy, and there are plenty of studies and research on both sides to build a case on either, but lately the research in favor of video games is so compelling that it's almost irresponsible to not acknowledge the many benefits that video games offer.

Who Plays Video Games?

When you think of gaming, you may picture a bunch of teen boys sitting in front of a big-screen TV like zombies, incessantly jamming buttons on their controllers, while aggressively playing violent video games.

This stereotype has been blown away by current research into what demographics play video games today. 2013 numbers from the Entertainment Software Association revealed that women have actually caught up, and the age groups that make up game players are well represented from 0 through 100 years old.

More recent numbers put men and women pretty much on equal footing as game players. This reality means that people from every walk of life and every age group turn to video games for their entertainment.

There is a reason so many people turn to gaming, and if recent research is any indication, it's because video games provide a tremendous vehicle for stress relief in anyone's life (plus, they're fun).

Video Games and Mental Health

A 2010 study at Texas A&M conducted by Associate Professor Dr. Christopher J. Ferguson showed that both men and women who play violent video games long-term seem to be able to adopt mental skills to handle stress, become less depressed and get less hostile during stressful tasks.

Ferguson's sample size was 103 students, and he explained the study as follows:

> "In this study, 103 young adults were given a frustration task and then randomized to play no game, a non-violent game, a violent game with good versus evil theme, or a violent game in which they played 'the bad guy.' The results suggest that violent games reduce depression and hostile feelings in players through mood management."

In fact, Ferguson suggested that violent video games could potentially be used as a form of therapy to help people find a way to "work through their frustrations" in real life.

For avid video gamers reading this, the results probably come as no surprise, considering that if you ask anyone you know who plays games why they play, a common answer is, "to relax" or "de-stress".

In fact when researchers at Massachusetts General Hospital polled children there about their video game playing habits, they discovered that a majority of kids choose to play video games as a way to manage difficult feelings like anger and stress.

Playing Video Games Will Help You De-Stress

In a 2014 study at University College in London, researchers surveyed 491 subjects and found a correlation between the total number of hours spent playing games (primarily first person shooters and action games) per week, and overall recovery from work-related stress that day.

Researchers Emily Collins and Anna L. Cox confirmed that there's a clear correlation between playing games and handling stress better, but also noted that there is not a proven causal relationship, because as they explain:

- "If an individual plays digital games, this may be due to the ability and inclination to take time to themselves and to pursue hobbies, and it may be this that reduces WHI and the need for recovery rather than the activity itself."

So, whatever the reason—if you make the conscious choice to play video games after work, you will experience faster recovery from the stress you experienced, and you'll be able to handle that stress all that much better the next day.

It isn't just children or young adults either. Researchers at the National Institute on Aging were so impressed by studies showing the positive effects of video games on cognitive functioning, that they launched a $1.2 million National Science Foundation (NSF) project to use a Nintendo Wii to try and help improve the daily cognitive functioning of senior citizens.

Okay....so maybe not *Mortal Kombat*....but you get the point.

Clearly, video games do have a direct, positive effect on the human brain. However, contrary to popular belief, the effects of video games are not negative, but positive.

In one 2009 study published in the *Journal of CyberTherapy & Rehabilitation*, researchers tested the effects of casual video games (CVGs) on gamers. The effects tested in this study included electroencephalography (EEG), and heart rate variability (HRV).

Since both of these physiological responses are used to indicate when someone is stressed, common sense would tell you that during video games that require a lot of attention (and often stressful, timed tasks), a person would end up more stressed than ever before!

The opposite was actually true. Researchers found that:

"Remarkably all three games had different yet complimentary mood lifting effects. BJW 2 decreased left alpha brain waves associated with a decrease in withdrawal and depressive type behaviors, and PGL increased right alpha brain wave activity associated with excitement or euphoric behaviors."

The final conclusion of the researchers was even more surprising. Not only did they suggest that gaming can help to reduce your stress, but they suggested using gaming as an actual form of therapy for people who suffer from various mental health issues.

"These findings have broad implications which include the potential development of prescriptive interventions using casual video games to prevent and treat stress related medical disorders."

This statement is plenty of vindication to convince anyone that taking a bit of time out of your day to play video games is very good for your mental and physical health.

These findings supported an earlier study from McGill University in 2007, when researchers found that playing what they called "social-intelligence games", reduced the stress hormone cortisol by an impressive 17 percent. It seems fairly obvious that if you play video games, you will not be as stressed out as you are right now.

Play Video Games at Least a Little Every Day

This research and the latest findings in this area of study have been enough to convince me to alter my daily schedule so that—in addition to going to the gym and working out at least 60 minutes a day—I am also scheduling in time to play some form of video games.

It seems like really anything will do—from action-packed first person shooters, to mind-challenging casual games online or on your mobile.

Do you play games to reduce your stress, if so, which ones reduce stress for you the most? If you don't play games, are you considering doing so now? Share your thoughts in the comments section below and let's discuss!

> "*Violent video games show kids how to express themselves physically, in a violent way. [...] My boys have their fair share of quarrels, but I don't want them to learn they should resolve conflicts by hurting each other.*"

How Violent Games are Bad for Your Kids

Laura St. John

In the following viewpoint, Laura St. John lays out the reasons why she, as a mother, feels violent video games are detrimental to kids: they offer a first-hand role in killing, they reward and measure success through killing, they teach disrespect for women, they have inappropriate language and sexual content, they desensitize killing and resolve conflicts through violence. Lastly, the author argues, violent games blur the line between fantasy and reality. St. John is an entrepreneur who runs a fitness company and is the mother of three sons.

As you read, consider the following questions:

1. Where does the author think a feeling of success should come from?
2. How does the author feel conflicts should be resolved?
3. Explain why the author thinks kids can't distinguish between reality and the fantasy in video games.

"8 Ways Violent Games Are Bad for Your Kids," by Laura St. John, Times Internet Limited, July 11, 2013. Reprinted by permission.

Life-changing. That sums up the reviews I read about Jane's game, *SuperBetter*. A personal life coach wrapped into a $4.99 app that is actually fun to play—and will change your life in a super better way. I nodded with excitement (and already added over 21 minutes to my life!) as I watched her TED video three times.

But if a game truly has the power to unlock such positivity on people's lives, it made me think about some of the other "what ifs" behind the power of gaming, especially its effect on the developing brain. So, what happens when we expose our kids—our next generation of leaders, cure-seekers, and innovators—to games that are not-so-super?

As a mom of three boys who like to shoot and blast things, and as co-creator of a wholesome game that teaches kids to solve real-world problems, my mind immediately worries about all the violent video games that are out there. You know, those "M" for Mature games that parents turn their backs to while the kids stay entertained for hours.

Here are eight ways that I found violent games are bad for your kids:

1. First-Hand Role in Killing Process.

To kids, virtual experiences feel very real, not only because the graphics today are so amazing, but because they are taking on a first-person role in the killing process. Rather than just passively watching a rated-R violent movie, when kids play a game, they are one of the main characters inside the adventure. The entire experience becomes a more meaningful—and deadly—in their brains, which are forming new connections every day.

2. Measure Success through Killing.

You know that "I did it!" feeling you get from Jane's SuperBetter game when you accomplish a mini task? A feeling of success should come from positive, challenging achievements—not the accomplishment of killing someone else. What kind of message is that sending to our kids?

GAMING ALTERS BRAINS

After playing violent video games for one week, young adult men showed signs of sustained changes in a region of the brain associated with emotional control, a new study shows.

This is the first time researchers at Indiana University—a group that has studied the effects of media violence for more than a decade—have conducted an experimental study that showed a direct relationship between playing violent video games over an extended period of time and a subsequent change in brain regions associated with cognitive function and emotional control.

[...] "For the first time, we have found that a sample of randomly assigned young adults showed less activation in certain frontal brain regions following a week of playing violent video games at home," says Yang Wang, assistant research professor of radiology and imaging sciences. "The affected brain regions are important for controlling emotion and aggressive behavior."

[...] "These findings indicate that violent video game play has a long-term effect on brain functioning," says Wang. "These effects may translate into behavioral changes over longer periods of game play."

"Guys' Brains Change After Violent Gaming," by Steve Chaplin, Futurity, December 6, 2011. Licensed Under CC BY-ND 4.0

3. Disrespect Women.

I am a pretty tough little chick: I live in a house filled with plenty of testosterone, and they all know not to mess with me. But majority of the ultra-violent games feature violence toward women. Now if some games can teach the habits of heroes, why would we ever harness the power of gaming to be mean toward me, or your girls—your daughters, my boys' future girlfriends?

4. Inappropriate Sexual Content.

Just like you wouldn't allow your child to go to or rent a rated R movie because of its inappropriate sexual content, many violent games are just as bad, if not worse. I don't know about you, but I don't want my kids learn about the birds and bees through a game.

5. Resolve Conflicts through Violence.

Violent video games show kids how to express themselves physically, in a violent way. It's already way easier for a child to push another child when they're angry than to express their emotions and resolve a conflict through words. My boys have their fair share of quarrels, but I don't want them to learn they should resolve conflicts by hurting each other.

6. De-Sensitizes Killing.

When you hear the tragic, heart-wrenching stories such as what happened in Newtown, Conn., you wonder how exposure to violent games de-sensitizes people to the act of killing other people. The thought of my little boys picking up a gun to shoot someone is not only disgusting, it teaches them to disrespect life. What if that could carry over to their own life or others? Ick, that makes me shudder.

7. Explicit Language.

The first time one of my sons was exposed to a violent game, I learned quickly that he was guilty after he said, "Oh, sh@#!" Enough said.

8. Fuzzy Line Between Real and Make-Believe.

Little kids have a hard time distinguishing the line between the real-world and the virtual gaming world, as young minds are still forming what is real and what is make-believe. I put it into perspective like this: If my kids believe in Santa or the Easter Bunny, then how could they possibly understand that these other bad guys in games, who look real, are not really real?

Now don't get me wrong: I am all for allowing kids plenty of screen time to be useful, productive, creative, and help make the world a better place. When used appropriately, technology has the power and potential to be the best tool ever invented. So now go use your power-ups for the greater good, and help make the world a SuperBetter place.

> *"The language used also seems to try to create sensation where there is none. In the section on violent reactions in real life, it admits that these are all imagined and not acted on."*

Interpretations of Video Game Studies Depend on Your Agenda

John Walker

In the following viewpoint, John Walker deconstructs a study that claims video gamers are unable to discern reality from fantasy. From interviews with a small group of teenagers, the researchers claim that their study shows that repeating a task many times in a game means the brain flickers on the idea of doing it in real life. Using a humorous and conversational tone, Walker cites many reasons why he feels the researchers fail to prove their point. Walker is a British computer games journalist, a cartoonist, and a TV critic.

As you read, consider the following questions:

1. What is Game Transfer Phenomena?
2. What does the author consider to be the most significant flaw of the study?
3. Why does John Walker discount the final conclusion of the research study?

Did you know that you can't tell reality from fantasy? No, I'm not a twenty-foot dragon from Saturn, silly! I'm a human. But you can't tell. I know this because the *Metro* told me so. According to the free rag, Nottingham Trent university researchers have revealed that gamers get so immersed in fantasy that they are unable to distinguish the real world. So this must be based on a broad, far-reaching study for the paper to make such a statement, right? No of course not. It's an interview study of 42 people. Which I've now read. And has nothing to do with the *Metro*'s conclusions. So obviously I'm going to take issue with the *Metro*'s coverage, but then get a little bit deeper when taking issue with the paper itself.

I don't mean to get all Ben Goldacre, but the wilful ignorance of newspaper coverage of science stories makes my brain hurt. This tiny proportion of people were selected on the basis of being aged between 15 and 21, and playing more than ten hours of games a week (an epic hour and 25 minutes a day). So not exactly a broad representation of anything, let alone gamers. It is, in fact, a study of teenagers, which doesn't get mentioned anywhere in the coverage.

So let's take a look at these examples of people losing the ability to distinguish reality.

> "One 15-year-old named Simon (the names used are not their real names) admitted wanting to use a 'gravity gun' from the game Half Life to fetch something from the fridge."

Er. Right. Who wouldn't? I want to be able to fly, or not need to wee. But I'm able to tell that these things aren't possible. There's no evidence shown to suggest that Simon believes that gravity guns are real, because he obviously doesn't.

> "Another gamer, Milton, 19, said when he dropped a sandwich after playing Prince Of Persia: Sands Of Time his finger 'twitched' as he tried to retrieve it with his console."

Ah, right, that's what they mean.

> "Linus, 19, said he thought he could use a search button in World of Warcraft when he tried to look for his older brother

in a crowd. Others said they unwittingly acted out situations inspired by games."

In other words, the research has discovered that repeating a task many times in a game means your brain flickers on the idea of doing it in real life. Of course! The number of times my brain has wanted to scroll up and down a magazine page, or been frustrated that wiggly red lines don't appear under spelling mistakes when I'm writing… But I'm fairly convinced I have a reasonable grip on the distinction between reality and fantasy, despite all that word processing I do.

So of course at this point it's time to actually look at the paper from which this is all drawn. And as one of the paper's authors, Dr. Mark Griffiths told us, these papers have their own agenda.

It is, in fact, a study of what they're calling Game Transfer Phenomena (GTP), where elements of gaming are associated with elements of real life, "triggering subsequent thoughts, sensations and/or player actions." These were grouped as either intentional or automatic experiences. The stated goal was not to prove that games are dangerous, but simply to study their Game Transfer Phenomenon with relation to understanding how immersion works.

Those interviewed were 42 Swedes (39 male, 3 female) between 15 and 21, who played a broad range of games regularly. And the incidents of these gaming ideas in their real life are really fun! Like the 19 year old who, when trying to find his brother in a crowd, considered using the /who function. Or the 17 year old who starts seeing walls and buildings as potential routes after playing lots of *Assassin's Creed*.

Which I think we can all quite anecdotally associate with that feeling of coming out of a big, action film at the cinema, and feeling like you could run incredibly fast, or lift up a car. These gamers report finding themselves looking at real life structures in the same way as they would in-game, looking for weaknesses or sniping points. It then goes on to describe the much-studied "Tetris effect" where you continue to see the shapes and patterns when you close your eyes, or in your dreams. Something that has proven absolutely essential for scientific research into dreaming since the 90s.

Things get more interesting when the paper discusses hypnagogic effects, such as imagining health bars above people's heads, or perceiving dialogue choices when in conversations. Neither of course suggests an inability to distinguish reality from fantasy, but instead makes for interesting study into the way fantasy can augment an understood reality. But then it all starts to look rather trivial again as the study reports examples of teenagers, well, playing. Hiding in a box like Solid Snake, talking like cowboys. Basically normal imitative behaviour.

The paper has a few distinct issues. One being a huge proportion of other papers cited were also co-authored by Griffiths. With an interest in so-called "gaming addiction", for which scant useful evidence actually exists, Griffiths is no stranger to gaming controversies. Although he has also published a number of papers recognising the broad range of benefits of gaming. It also makes rather liberal use of the word "perhaps", every time it wants to make an unsubstantiated claim.

> "Today's video games have evolved due to technological advance, resulting in high levels of realism and emotional design that include diversity, experimentation, and (perhaps in some cases) sensory overload."

Regarding the claims of dissociation, the paper itself identifies this as "fuzzy", pointing out that there's "no clear accepted definition of what it actually constitutes." It then goes on to fudge a rather ambiguous association with gaming, seemingly deliberately ignoring the trauma aspects one would more usually associate with dissociative behaviour.

It's also a little troubling that there's a seeming lack of familiarity with the games being discussed. The typographical error, "When just 'Cause 2' got released…" is telling.

But most significantly, and of course a typical flaw in interview-based research, is that the psychological profiles of those taking part were not looked into, let alone taken into account (as the paper goes on to discuss in its discussion). One subject referred to as Linus, aged 19, contributes some of the more extreme responses (such as dancing like a WoW character in his school), and "Carl", also 19, who reports that he has brief urges (on which he does not act) to throw himself down stairways and steal cars. Because only 42 were studied, and because they were selected from Swedish gaming forums without any psychological profiling, such anecdotes are pretty much useless out of context. Perhaps "Carl" does suffer from delusions and dissociation, and games aren't helping him (although the evidence given here suggests not, just that he recalls gaming actions in real life before dismissing them). But we don't know, and there's certainly no proof, nor any attempt to prove, that gaming would be the cause of this. Terms like "intrusive thoughts"—a condition associated with anxiety disorders—are used astonishingly inappropriately here, again without evidence.

The language used also seems to try to create sensation where there is none. In the section on violent reactions in real life, it admits that these are all imagined and not acted on. But almost reluctantly, with language like,

> "Violent solutions to real life conflicts appeared to be used by
> a few of the players, at least in their imaginations."

That's just abysmal phrasing in a scientific paper, almost as bad as the newspapers so lazily misquoting it all. It should more properly read, "Violent solutions to real life conflicts were not used by players, but some imagined doing so."

I also find the paper's use of the word "even" to be extremely unhelpful. Repeatedly it editorialises with this word to imply more than is being reported. For instance,

> "Some players reported that their perception of the world had
> changed, at least temporarily, when they found themselves
> integrating dangerous scenarios in the real life environment.
> Most of the time these experiences appeared as a thought, but one
> player even performed an action to avoid the possible danger."

Again the phrasing sensationalises before admitting the reality. And the use of "even" is entirely unnecessary—this is supposed to be reporting findings, not being astonished by them. And the incident? It's Linus again, who said that he once chose to stick to the path when walking through some woods, because he's "less likely to get attacked my [sic] mobs."

It's also not helpful that they conclude that imagined things were "hallucinations", which is an extremely strong word to describe seeing floating images after staring at a repeated pattern for a long time. Such exaggeration reaches the point of farce when the discussion of uncanny moments of associating games with life is described as opening "a 'Pandora's Box' for some players". Yes, thinking that a street looks a bit like *Assassin's Creed* is very much the same as unleashing all the evil forces in the universe.

Perhaps the most strange and heavily biased aspect of the study comes in what the researchers choose to dismiss. Gamers reporting to them that they can distinguish reality from fantasy even during the GTP events is dismissed, based on other things the gamers said. Which makes no sense at all. Because the researchers conclude these anecdotes are examples of hallucinations, delusions, etc, with no psychological evidence, it is considered that this contradicts the gamers' statements that they are able to distinguish such moments. Why not the other way around? This is not considered. Nor is the similarity of these effects with watching television or film. Clearly this is a study of gaming, but to not mention that the same effects are commonplace from other media is willfully ignorant.

Of course the study does go on to list its own flaws, as is only proper. It acknowledges that the sample size was extremely small, and that "the findings cannot be generalized in a mechanical way." It also mentions that the questions used in the interviews (most of which were electronic) "may have influenced the experiences reported by the players and the incidence of certain experiences."

And its final conclusion? "Modern video games' realistic scenarios may trigger associations between the two worlds among some individuals." Aside from the complete failure to explore the concept of "realistic scenarios" at any point during the study, indeed referencing *Tetris* and *Guitar Hero* as often as GTA or *Assassin's Creed*, and that making such a conclusion is mystifying, it's rather important to note that this does not, in any sense, suggest that gamers cannot tell the real world from fantasy, as the Metro newspaper claims.

Of course, it's worth noting the Metro's agenda here. The "Related Items" bar at the side lists the following headlines in order:

"'*Call Of Duty* makes gamers dumb' says Dishonoured developer"

"Nintendo 3DS 'makes gamers sick'"

"Teenage gamer hangs himself in 'virtual suicide mistake'"

It's taking all my strength not to pick apart the nonsense in each of those three stories too. And of course on the other side of the screen are the newspaper's links to its Gamescom 2011 coverage. Gosh, it will eat all of that cake. Perhaps they're best off sticking to reporting how Nic Cage is a vampire.

Then of course there's the Mail's approach to the story, where they use it as proof that GTA caused the killing on that submarine.

Periodical and Internet Sources Bibliography

The following articles have been selected to supplement the diverse views presented in this chapter.

Nick Bilton "Looking at Link Between Violent Video Games and Lack of Empathy," *Bits,* June 15, 2014.

Greg Bump "Study finds violent video games provide quick stress relief, but at a price," *W News,* July 9, 2015.

Tracy Clark-Flory "Study: Sexist, Violent Video Games Decrease Empathy in Boys," *Vocativ,* April 13, 2016.

Mark Denicola "Are Video Games Actually Desensitizing Us to Violence?" *Collective Evolution,* November 21, 2014.

Serena Gordon "Violent Video Games May Not Desensitize Kids," *U.S. News & World Report,* February 23, 2011.

Emily Hughes "Effects of Video Games on Child Development," *Developmental Psychology at Vanderbilt,* April 24, 2014.

Alex Layne "Empathy and Video Games," *Not Your Mama's Gamer,* March 24, 2016.

Brendan J. McCollum "Violent Video Games and Symptoms of Distress and Trauma," *Georgia Southern University,* Spring, 2014.

Keith Simmons "EverQuest: Blurring the Lines Between Reality and Fantasy," *Standford University,* 2003.

Jonathan Strickland "Does violence in movies and video games desensitize us to the real thing?" *How Stuff Works,* August 24, 2010.

CHAPTER 3

Can Violent Video Games Lead to Extreme or Criminal Behavior?

Chapter Preface

Extremes and violence often go together, and violent video games are no exception.

Almost without fail, every mass shooting in recent history has been blamed on the fact that the shooter played violent video games. Yet, 97% of teens in America play video games; more than half of them contain some form of violent content. Are all these teens mass shooters? Of course not. But the question is, are some kids actually influenced by the violence in these games enough to kill in real life?

There is evidence that violent games have sometimes played a part in the lives of mass shooters, such as the students who modeled themselves after the shooters in *Doom*. But experts don't agree that this is the only factor in how these kids became killers. So, are young people influenced by violence in games and are the games teaching them how? And why have crime rates gone down as video game sales have gone up?

Bullying has probably existed as long as people have, but lately, in America, it has been represented in the media as almost epidemic and in some instances, has led to suicide. Is there a connection to kids playing violent video games? One study claims a direct connection between "highly violent" video games and kids being more likely to bully their peers. Others claim there is no connection.

A relatively new word (coined in 2001) is now a part of our culture: cyberbullying, or bullying online. While it incorporates all social media, it can definitely play a part in many of the violent video games. MMO's (massively multiplayer online games) provide a platform for cooperative video game play. But they also provide a stage for online bullying. Do the games incite kids to cyberbully or are they just a convenient vehicle into which bullying neatly fits? Would these kids bully others if they didn't use video games?

And does the bullying extend to the actual players outside of the game parameters?

In the following chapter, the authors argue for and against violent video games as they relate to mass murders, bullying and cyberbullying.

> "As the writers themselves admit,
> hidden right down the bottom of
> their conclusion like a murmured
> confession, the findings of the
> study do not in any way show any
> connection between the playing of
> violent videogames and a likelihood
> of committing gun crimes."

Video Games Don't Make Deadly Shooters

Brendan Keogh

In the following viewpoint, Brendan Keogh contends that the media's portrayal of a study conducted to research a connection between violent video games and gun violence did not at all reflect the real results of the study. He recounts details of the study and argues that the media's spin on it was misleading and irresponsible. He further relates that the study shows that video games can train people how to shoot but not that they would actually shoot someone in a real-life situation. Keogh is a a PhD candidate whose research concerns how we experience and understand videogame play, as well as a videogame critic and journalist for a variety of publications.

"Bite the Bullet: videogames don't make deadly shooters," by Brendan Keogh, The Conversation, June 5, 2012. https://theconversation.com/bite-the-bullet-videogames-dont-make-deadly-shooters-7346. Licensed under CC BY-ND 4.0.

As you read, consider the following questions:

1. What two results did the study actually find?
2. Describe the two types of controllers and how they affect the results of the study.
3. What is the author's issue with this study and its accompanying press release?

I s there an explicit link between playing violent videogames and becoming a deadly killer? If we are to take seriously a new study published in the journal *Communication Research*, there seems to be.

Cue tabloid headlines of the sort: "Is the Xbox Turning Your Child Into A Deadly Shooter?"

Maybe such articles will also casually mention the 1999 Columbine Massacre, in which 13 people were killed by two students who just so happened to play videogames.

Or maybe they'll feature a photo of Anders Breivik because he mentioned playing *Modern Warfare 2* (after all, we took everything else he said seriously, right?).

Such articles won't feature any critical engagement or scrutiny of the actual complexities of videogame play—just more mind-numbing nods to another simplistic study, yet again seeming to prove violent videogames make players into killers.

Actually, this isn't what the study—conducted by Jodi L. Whitaker and Brad H. Bushman of the University of Michigan—has shown at all, but it sure does sound good in a press release.

Which is probably what prompted several smaller science news websites to copy-paste the press release as "news". One of those was accompanied by a photo of the game *Modern Warfare 2*, which actually has nothing to do with what the study actually found, as we'll see below.

Another website bothered to find a third party who noted that the methods and findings of the paper are, at best, incredulous. Sadly, this insight was followed by a random reference to, yes, the

Columbine Massacre. The story also featured an image of a young boy in camouflage with a plastic gun and knife. Classy.

To be fair, the headline of the study's press release (put together by SAGE Publications, the publisher of *Communication Research*) set the tone:

> "Violent video games turning gamers into deadly shooters"

This is only marginally more deceptive and slanted than the actual paper, which takes the quote in the headline, "Boom, Headshot!", from FPS Doug, a fictional character from the fictional web-series Pure Pwnage. Somewhat ironically, the authors seem oblivious to the fact that Pure Pwnage is a show that satirises the popular image of the pro-gamer with exaggerated, self-conscious stereotypes.

Such (lack of) judgement doesn't help me shake my initial suspicions that the authors were more concerned with proving their own assumptions about video games and gamers than they were about expanding any particular body of knowledge.

Regardless of what the paper did or didn't find, it comes across as construed and misleading. Unfortunately this tends to be the rule rather than the exception when it comes to research on video games.

What the study actually found is far less exciting than the flourished press release would have us believe:

1. simulations with replicated hardware can help train mechanical and physical skills

2. players who play violent videogames are more likely to aim for the head when playing a game with a gun—be it digital or otherwise—than elsewhere on the body.

The first point hardly counts as a point at all. The second is interesting, certainly, but not the causal link to violent action implied by the study and the accompanying press release.

The authors had 151 college students spend 20 minutes playing one of three videogames: *Resident Evil 4* (referred to throughout the paper simply as "a violent shooting game"); the target practice

MENTAL ILLNESS AS COMMON THREAD IN MASS MURDER

The killers responsible for the murders at Columbine, Aurora, and Sandy Hook reportedly played a lot of video games, although the shooter at Virginia Tech did not. Yet, the Sandy Hook killer mostly played nonviolent games (he spent the most time playing *Super Mario Brothers* and *Dance Dance Revolution*), and the shooter at Aurora played mostly role-playing games (fantasy-based games that feature armed combat against primarily monsters) like *World of Warcraft*, *Neverwinter Nights*, and *Diablo*, which do not feature guns. Of all the perpetrators of these horrific mass shootings, only the Columbine shooters actually played games that involve using guns to shoot people. The more common thread? All were mentally ill at the time of the shootings and all had access to guns. [...]

Video games could have been part of their illness, of course. Suffering from a serious psychosis conceivably could lead to seeking out experiences and media that reinforce that psychosis and color one's perceptions of what those experiences mean. But it is another thing entirely to reverse the order and suggest that the medium or the experiences caused the illness.

"What Can We Learn from Violent Video Games?" by Richard Van Eck, Educause Review, October 12, 2015.

mini game in Wii Play ("a nonviolent shooting game"); or *Super Mario Galaxy* ("a nonviolent, non-shooting game").

Afterwards, the subjects took 16 pot shots at a mannequin at a shooting range. The mannequin was placed close enough, the writers note, that the subjects would most probably hit whichever part of the body they chose to aim for.

Most significantly, the subjects who played one of the shooting games were split into two further groups. These sub groups played the game in question with two different types of controllers. One group played with traditional controllers with joysticks and buttons, while the other played with a light-gun controller. That is, a controller shaped like a gun that the player must accurately aim at the targets on the television in order to shoot them.

The findings are hardly surprising. Players that used a "real" gun controller to shoot humanoid enemies in *Resident Evil 4* were more accurate at the shooting range than those using a standard controller. Likewise, those that played Wii Play with the "real" gun controller were also more accurate than those that played with a standard controller.

What is more interesting, though, is that those subjects that played *Resident Evil 4* were more likely to aim for the head than those that played any other game, regardless of controller type.

Let's deal first with the controllers. Video games that use light gun controllers have existed for decades, and have been popular in arcades with series such as *Time Crisis, Virtua Cop,* and *House of the Dead.* Such games continue a much older carnival tradition of shooting galleries.

Sometimes the targets are simple targets, but often the player takes the first-person role of a good guy running through corridors, gunning down bad guys. In such games the player's character is normally pushed along a linear path with no control over movement (giving them the nickname "on-rails shooters") and the player's only task is shooting accurately and quickly.

Light-gun games have also appeared on home consoles, but to a far-lesser extent due to the need of specialist controllers and spacious living rooms. The Nintendo Wii, however, has been particularly well-suited for bringing the genre back as the native Wii-mote controllers already shoot infra-red lasers at the TV and only require a cheap gun-shaped plastic holder for the controller to be placed into.

These light-gun games are a perfect example of what I've previously labelled synecdochic controllers: the action the player performs in the actual world closely mirrors the action of the character in the fictional world—in this case, aiming and shooting a gun.

That synecdochic controllers such as light guns could train users in the use of firearms is hardly a surprise. You hold the gun the same way as a real gun. You aim and pull the trigger like a real gun. I know of no light guns that give players a realistic lesson in recoil, reloading, bullet-drop, flicking the safety switch, or other essential elements of effective firearm use, but it certainly wouldn't be hard to design a light gun and a simulation that did teach these things.

Regardless, the current model light guns unarguably train users how to aim a firearm-shaped tool. It's a replication and a simulation. Driving and flying schools have been doing this for decades. Attach a video simulation to the mechanical hardware you want the student to master, and you have a safe environment for them to practise.

The claim that light gun games can train players to better use firearms is hardly contentious. But I have a problem with the misleading conflation of "light-gun games" and "violent videogames". This is a gross inaccuracy when you consider what a minor percentage of videogames actually use light guns.

In contrast to the synecdochic light gun, the vast majority of shooting games use metonymic controllers that are more metaphorical in their translation of actual-world action into the fictional world.

Guns are aimed with joysticks and buttons, or with keyboards and mice. You move the camera around until the crosshair overlaps with the targets, and then you press a button to fire. In most videogames that include shooting, the actual-world action of the player has little if any similarities with the functional use of a firearm (though this is complicated when the US Army starts designing drones with controls meant to replicate videogame controllers).

Perhaps replicated firearm usage can train more proficient firearm users, but that is hardly proof that "violent video games" are turning players into "deadly shooters".

Unarguably, shooting video games that use metonymic controls can teach players theoretical things about combat and firearm usage—I wouldn't even know what "bullet-drop" was were it not for videogames! (In case you were wondering, bullet-drop is essentially the effect of gravity on the fired bullet).

The US army uses its own custom-built game, America's Army, to teach players how to work as a squad, how different pieces of equipment (from firearms to vehicles) actually work, and (most importantly) how to sign up and join the real army.

But beyond the theoretical or ideological, to teach a practical, physical, applicable skill with a video game you would need a practical, applicable, synecdochic controller—a mechanical device which acts functionally similar to the real-world counterpart.

Considering that so few violent video games use light guns (never mind the fact that not all "violent" video games even depict shooting), it's quite a stretch to say Whitaker and Bushman's study proves any connection with violent videogames in general and firearm efficiency.

At worst, the accompanying press release—unlikely to have been written by the study's authors—was a malicious attempt to grab some easy attention by hinting at a fraudulent but popular connection between violent video games and gun crimes. At best, the study comes across as a lazy simplification of what video games do, with little interrogation of how they actually function.

I personally suspect the latter and members of the video games industry are deserving of at least some of the blame for such a persistently inaccurate depiction. After all, with the way video games are depicted on television and in films, someone who does not engage with the culture could easily be forgiven for thinking that the vast majority of violent video games put "real" guns into players hands.

Take this particularly absurd example (see video below) from the fourth season of AMC's *Breaking Bad*. Id's software's game *Rage* for the Microsoft Xbox 360 is depicted multiple times throughout the season in what is almost certainly an intentional product placement campaign.

At one point, the character Jesse is shown playing the game, standing in his lounge room with a light gun, blasting mutants and having flashbacks from a real-life gun crime he committed, unable to differentiate the two.

The thing is, *Rage* doesn't use a light gun. At all. There is no version of the game that does. At some point, Microsoft, Id Software, or the game's publisher, Bethesda, must have OK-ed this scene, knowing *Rage* would be depicted as using a light gun even though it only ever uses a typical controller. Worse is the fact the scene would claim the player, Jesse, couldn't differentiate between shooting mutants and actual people.

It's obvious why the show wanted a light-gun version of *Rage*—Jesse sitting on his couch with a controller would be far less involving, far less emotive. The viewers want to see Jesse actually doing what he is doing in the game.

But still, when a video game company apparently agrees to have its game misrepresented as something done with real guns by meth addicts who can't differentiate gameplay from gun crime, who can blame the mass media or the psychological studies? The video game industry and culture shoots itself in the foot. Or, perhaps more appropriately, the head.

Which brings us back to the one interesting (and perhaps chilling) finding the study in *Communication Research* does make. Not only were those subjects that used a light gun more accurate than those that used a traditional controller, those that played *Resident Evil 4* (either with a light gun or with a traditional controller) were more likely to shoot at a mannequin's head than anywhere else on the body. This seems to suggest that the game's temperament of rewarding headshots influenced which part of the mannequin subjects subsequently aimed at.

It's true, as the study notes, that many shooting games do reward the player for aiming at the head. Sometimes this reward is intrinsic: maybe enemies die quicker from headshots (thus allowing a player to conserve ammunition) or maybe their heads explode in a visually satisfying way.

But headshots also often result in extra in-game points or medals. The 2010 entry in the *Medal of Honor* series, for instance, while attempting to treat (western) soldiers with respect and sobriety (the movie opens with the sombre "They shall grow not old, as we that are left grow old" verse from Laurence Binyon's "For the Fallen"), it rewards players with a medal every time they shoot an enemy in the head.

It's a weird, jarring design choice which only seems to be there because video games need to acknowledge headshots.

Perhaps the proliferation and glorification of headshots in video games can be situated in a much broader media context, where films, television series, and novels have all romanticised and glorified firearm accuracy generally and headshots specifically.

Many action films, such as *Bad Boys II*, end with the good guys dramatically and stylishly ending the bad guy with a headshot, while the depiction of Legolas's accuracy with his bow in Lord of the Rings is treated as nothing less than poetry. It speaks to both the majestic, superhuman aim of the shooter and the utterly conclusive death of the victim.

Whitaker and Bushman's study certainly seems to show that players took their motivation to aim for the head from the video game to the shooting range. Still, I am not convinced this proves what part of the body these subjects would aim at if confronted with a situation where they had to shoot at a real human. Perhaps they saw the shooting range as just another (non-digital) game with humanoid targets.

After all, if a shooting range has human-shaped targets, it's not uncommon for those targets to have bullseyes on the forehead. It's unfortunate the study's authors didn't also get subjects to practise at the shooting gallery for 20 minutes, too, to compare this with the subjects' skill transferal from playing video games.

My issue with the article (and even more so its accompanying press release) is its unethical presentation, its seeming eagerness to hide its actual findings beneath a rhetorical perspective that reaffirms and strengthens the inaccurate and simplistic view the mass media loves to perpetuate that video games are evil murder simulators.

As the writers themselves admit, hidden right down the bottom of their conclusion like a murmured confession, the findings of the study do not in any way show any connection between the playing of violent video games and a likelihood of committing gun crimes or any other violent act:

"Playing the violent shooting game facilitated the learning of shooting behavior but does not necessarily make it more likely that the player would actually fire a real gun."

They merely show practising with a replicated gun might improve a subject's accuracy if the situation arose where they had to fire a real gun. But this is a conclusion far removed from the flamboyant press release's call to "deadly shooters" or the fictional gamer's cry of "Boom, headshot!" that crowns the article's title.

Understanding how players engage with video games and violence that is simultaneously depicted and enacted is a crucial avenue of enquiry. But video games are complicated things. No less than films. No less than novels. No less than any other form of media people engage with.

It's about time researchers acknowledged this instead of seeking easy, linear and lazy cause-and-effect models that insult the multitudes of people that play video games.

> *"A coordinated bullying attack can result in an onslaught of threatening and harassing messages being sent to the kid who gets bullied. Victims will either stop playing the game altogether or they will deflect the harassment and begin bullying other gamers on their own."*

Violent Video Games: A Place for Cyberbullying

Jesse Aaron

In the following viewpoint, Jesse Aaron makes a case for why violent video games have become a perfect venue for cyberbullying. Of course, the internet and social media are breeding grounds for bulling, but there the aggressive and competitive culture of video games can take cyberbulling one step further. In his argument, the author describes the different types of cyberbullies and addresses his views on why they bully, as well as offering his solution. Aaron is a writer and blogger whose work has appeared on Yahoo!, Small Business Adviser, Social Media Examiner, and others.

"Cyber-bullying and video games," by Jesse Aaron, VentureBeat, September 26, 2014. Reprinted by permission.

As you read, consider the following questions:

1. Why does the author feel that bullies "flock to cyberspace"?
2. What are the reasons he cites for cyberbullying?
3. What is his solution to cyberbullying?

The saying goes, "kids will be kids." But what does the life of a modern kid in American, European, and Asian countries share?

Internet access.

Bullying—the physical, school-ground kind—has actually been classified as a public health issue. It wasn't until the mid-90s where instances of cyber-bullying garnered enough attention to warrant a subset classification, primarily because the effects of cyber-bullying were either identical or more severe than physical bullying. These include emotional stress, self-harm, and in rare cases, murder or suicide.

Despite the fact that socially conscious parents and politicians have been pushing for anti-bullying laws, it appears as though the anonymity that the Internet provides is giving bullies another outlet to harass their prey. It's common for bullies to flock to cyberspace and online video games to harass others. It's convenient for them. The prevalence is so great that the sheer amount of public backlash is reason enough to assume every gamer has experienced cyber-bullying at least once in their life.

There are many different types of cyber-bullying specific to video games, which include:

Role-playing games

In many online games, gamers will take on personas as they conquer their enemies and get stronger. As their characters get more violent and more advanced, many of these gamers might take on some of the less appealing characteristics of these personas, bullying their opponents without even realizing it. Because these kinds of games are very addicting, bullies and those who are bullied are likely to keep signing on in the face of degrading social situations.

Harassing messages

Some kids think it's okay to send harassing messages to their opponents in the online gaming world. After all, it's not real life—it's just a game. "You're protected by anonymity." Even if kids are nice in "real life," the anonymity that is provided on online gaming platforms emboldens them to be able to act disgustingly. These bullies don't understand that oftentimes, the harassing messages sent through cyberspace can have the same kind of impact on them as hurtful comments given in real life.

Ganging up

With their powers combined, bullies can more easily target their prey. A coordinated bullying attack can result in an onslaught of threatening and harassing messages being sent to the kid who gets bullied. Victims will either stop playing the game altogether or they will deflect the harassment and begin bullying other gamers on their own.

Griefers

Believe it or not, there are some people who play online video games for the sheer "satisfaction" of harassing other players. These bullies might even be sick adults who are seeking to target younger insecure kids. On top of harassing their targets inside the game, many of these griefers will also figure out how to harass them outside of the game—through various forms of manipulation (such as acquiring cell phone numbers)—and sending them threatening text messages. The goal of these individuals is to make the gaming experience as awful for their targets as possible.

Password theft

Some bullies will spend their time trying to figure out their target's password or hack into that person's account. Once inside, these bullies can wreak havoc by sending a slew of messages that will appear to be sent from the victim when in fact they are not. Hackers can subsequently change the password of the account, meaning the victim is no longer able to access it, excluding that person from being able to interact with his or her peers.

Viruses

Hackers can also choose to infect their target's gaming systems of computers with viruses. Many online gaming platforms and social networks, for example, have chat boxes built into them. As such, nefarious individuals can paste links to viruses, malware and spyware in them. Unsuspecting individuals could click on the disguised links, and next thing they know, their computers could be working improperly.

Why do bullies, bully?

43% of teens aged 13-17 have reported an experience where they were cyber bullied. But for video game players, that percentage could be significantly higher. In fact, 63% of female gamers have been sexually harassed (in digital environments), such as being asked to perform "virtual sex behaviors" in return for in-game currencies.

Interestingly, the primary reasons for cyberbullying are most likely false ideations of "someone deserving it." Maybe a victim published their honest thoughts in a forum that criticized a "guild" or the community of a game. Just look at the MOBA communities, specifically *League of Legends* and *Dota*. They're extremely volatile—that's an undeniable fact. If you run a Google search about either community, you'll find thousands upon thousands of rants, outcries, and criticisms.

It seems the only practical "solution" to cyber-bullying in video-game context is education and enforcement from both parents and developers. Teens are granted unrestricted social abilities with the mask of anonymity, but schools and parents hardly acknowledge this as a power—let alone something that can easily be abused and hurt kids (or their own).

> *"Might the characters in the games themselves, and by extension those who make them, also be encouraging bullying?"*

Changing Video Games Could Stop Bullying
Patrick Stafford

In the following viewpoint, Patrick Stafford discusses the emotional abuse that takes place between players in online gaming, specifically bullying in the form of threats and sexual harassment. The author cites research conducted by writer Rosalind Wiseman and actor Ashly Burch in which they conclcuded that the hero of one of the most-played videogames is cold and emotionless, a trait that leads to hurtful expression online in the form of racism, homophobia, and misogyny. Their proposition to game creators? Make the characters better role models, still strong and brave, but also empathetic. Stafford is a journalist based in Melbourne, Australia.

As you read, consider the following questions:

1. What is the main problem the author is attempting to solve in this article?
2. What did Wiseman and Burch learn from their research study of school-aged boys?
3. What action do they think game makers could take to mitigate online bullying?

The claim that video games cause young boys to be violent or abusive has been largely discredited. But it speaks the truth loudly when reversed: Video games are where boys go to be horrible.

Tales of emotional abuse between players in online games are so common as to be cliché at this point. The Internet is filled with stories of young men sending disgusting and violent threats, both verbally and though private messaging systems, mostly targeted at girls. Sexual harassment is common.

As just one example: A 2013 study from Ohio University found that when a female player in *Halo 3* greeted other players with an innocuous phrase like "hi everyone"—with no other information— she faced replies like "shut up you whore." A rallying cry of "alright team let's do this" earned the response, "slut."

The problem has become so dire it has prompted corporate response. Microsoft even created a new type of system for reporting player harassment and behavior for the Xbox One console, released late last year.

Many observers have said that this sort of behavior is inherent in virtual competitive environments, where players are for the most part anonymous. Others say boys will be boys. But might the characters in the games themselves, and by extension those who make them, also be encouraging bullying?

That's the question Rosalind Wiseman, best known for her book *Queen Bees and Wannabees* (the basis for *Mean Girls*), and actor Ashly Burch, of the successful gaming-focused web series "Hey Ash Whatcha Playin,'" have been investigating. The idea that game makers have a responsibility for abusive player behavior is a controversial one, but Wiseman and Burch say that a few less-than-drastic changes on designers' part could help make gaming a friendlier place.

Rosalind started looking into the topic while working on her recent book on raising boys, Masterminds and Wingmen. To help research, she teamed up with Burch, who had temporarily quit video games a few years ago due to harassment from other players.

At a talk at the annual Game Developer's Conference in March, Wiseman and Burch showed the results of some research they conducted, asking 200 school-aged boys about what they believe to be the most desirable traits for a man.

It's typical stuff—boys want to be seen as strong, with good verbal skills. Smart but not too smart, athletic at the right sports, able to spend some money. They don't get emotional, they're not nerdy, and they're certainly not sappy.

In a separate survey of more than 1,000 boys, Wiseman and Burch asked about video-game habits. Overwhelmingly, the boys chose Master Chief, the hero of Microsoft's blockbuster *Halo* series, as their favorite character.

Why? He's a "badass," according to the kids, "an amalgamation of all the things boys want to be," Burch says. "They want to be cool and save the day."

The problem with that, Burch says, is that Master Chief is emotionless, a point she emphasized at GDC by showing footage of a climactic scene in which Master Chief sounded like a robot.

The highest-grossing games feature similarly unfeeling men at their center: *BioShock Infinite*, *Call of Duty*, and *Grand Theft Auto V*. Hints of vulnerability are few and far between. (Tellingly, the one game in which the protagonist regularly revealed their pain and fear of failure had a woman in the spotlight: *Tomb Raider*.)

These heroes' coldness isn't necessarily the source of any bad behavior, but Wiseman argues when boys lack other solid role models, game characters' emotional distance can serve as an example to follow. That in turn allows boys to default to hurtful expression online: racism, homophobia and misogyny. If feelings aren't cool, you're not worried about hurting them, right?

Although Wiseman admits there isn't yet research that shows empathy in media characters can influence behavior, one 2007 study published in the journal *Developmental Psychology* showed promise. Researchers at the University of Michigan and VU University Amsterdam found boys who identified with violent characters were more likely to be violent in real life. They also pinpointed the possibility of the reverse being true: "Future research should also investigate the role of empathy in violent video game effects."

It's tempting to ignore boys' online behavior as inconsequential, but Wiseman points out that today's abusive teenagers turn into tomorrow's men. And those men are just as bad. After all, with the average age of male gamers over 30, many abusive players are likely to be adults.

That's why Wiseman and Burch say game makers should feel obligated, as creators of the most popular entertainment medium for boys, to inject some emotional nuance into their work.

Making cooperation a part of gameplay is an easy way to do that. Many games already require players to use teamwork to win, but Burch and Wiseman say more can be done. Football matches require players to shake hand after every match—what if there was a digital equivalent?

More studios, aware of the impact abusive players can have on their reputation, are attempting to curb this type of behavior. Riot Games, maker of the multiplayer strategy game *League of Legends*, which has more than 55 million users, has poured huge amounts of money into finding solutions to encourage sportsmanship.

Jeffrey Lin, head of social systems at Riot Games, suggests early efforts have worked. Taking away chat functionality from players who receive multiple negative reports can reverse bad behavior, for example.

Cooperation and politeness are the norm in many e-sports already. Starting a game of the real-time strategy title *StarCraft* begins more often than not with a customary message of "GLHF": Good luck, have fun.

Creating heroes who actually display emotion, fear, and even moments in which they have no idea what the hell they're doing can be a relief for young men, Wiseman says. A key idea of her most recent book is that boys have rich emotional lives, and don't really want to be constrained by the old, repressive stereotypes of masculinity.

"The boys I know don't want stoic dads," she says. "They want courageous, strong dads, but they want them to admit moments of weakness and fear."

Pop culture has already started reflecting that idea on TV and in film, where strong-silent types have given way to more fully human leading males. Think of Daniel Craig's wounded take on James Bond, or Robert Downey Jr.'s PTSD-affected Iron Man, both of whom have real, warm relationships with others.

Gaming hasn't caught up, but there are signs it could. Telltale's *The Walking Dead*, one of the most critically acclaimed game series of 2013, featured a black man as the protagonist—a rarity in games—who regularly was forced to make harrowing decisions and confront his own shortcomings. Does he reveal the truth about his past as a convicted murderer to his new companions—or risk them finding out on their own with dire consequences?

It's the player's choice, but for the most part, Lee is a benevolent character, taking an orphaned girl under his stewardship and often putting himself in danger to protect her.

Of course, this characterization isn't available in multiplayer environments, which is where most abuse takes place. Burch says this is why it's so important to reinforce cooperation between players: Why couldn't we show an animation of players in a first-person shooter patting each other on the back after a game, she asks?

Some in the games industry aren't convinced. In March, an audience member at Wiseman and Burch's developers talk posed a question that exemplified the very problem they're trying to fix: Wouldn't their suggestions essentially make Master Chief "into a girl"?

Wiseman responded calmly to the sexist assumptions embedded in the question: "What Ashly and I are asking you to do is create heroes that allow children to look at themselves and say, 'I can be Master Chief—male or female—but I can also ask for help, and admit how important the relationships are in my life.'"

"Our results indicated that violent video games were associated with neither delinquent criminality nor bullying behaviors in children with either clinically elevated depressive or attention deficit symptoms."

Study Finds No Impact of Violent Video Games on Bullying

Christopher J. Ferguson and Cheryl K. Olson

In the following viewpoint, Christopher J. Ferguson and Cheryl K. Olson review a study that sought to determine whether or not children with pre-existing mental health problems were adversely affected by playing violent video games. The results of this study of 377 children, mean age 12.93 years, did not support the hypothesis that children with mental health issues are more vulnerable to the effects of violence in video games than children without mental health issues. Ferguson is a professor of psychology at Stetson University, DeLand, Florida whose research focuses on media effects on children. Olson is the co-founder and co-director of the Center for Mental Health and Media at Massachusetts General Hospital and researches public health and policy related to media issues.

"Video Game Violence Use Among 'Vulnerable' Populations: The Impact of Violent Games on Delinquency and Bullying Among Children with Clinically Elevated Depression or Attention Deficit Symptoms," by Christopher J. Ferguson, Cheryl K. Olson, Springer International Publishing AG, August 24, 2013. Reprinted by permission.

As you read, consider the following questions:

1. On what premise was this study conducted?
2. What specific factors were considered in the "regression equation"?
3. What were the results of this study in regard to bullying?

Abstract

The issue of children's exposure to violent video games has been a source of considerable debate for several decades. Questions persist whether children with pre-existing mental health problems may be influenced adversely by exposure to violent games, even if other children are not. We explored this issue with 377 children (62 % female, mixed ethnicity, mean age = 12.93) displaying clinically elevated attention deficit or depressive symptoms on the Pediatric Symptom Checklist. Results from our study found no evidence for increased bullying or delinquent behaviors among youth with clinically elevated mental health symptoms who also played violent video games. Our results did not support the hypothesis that children with elevated mental health symptoms constitute a "vulnerable" population for video game violence effects. Implications and suggestions for further research are provided.

[...]

Bullying

The Revised Olweus Bully/Victim Questionnaire (Olweus 1996) was used to assess bullying behaviors. The bullying perpetration scale consisted of 9 items in which participants were asked to rate how often they had engaged in bullying behaviors over the past couple of months. Items inquire about physical aggression, verbal aggression, threats and social exclusion. A coefficient alpha of .86 was obtained for the current sample. The sample reported mean was 2.68 and standard deviation was 4.27.

Procedure

All procedures described within this study were approved by local IRB and designed to comport with APA standards for ethical human research. An "opt out" procedure was used for student involvement, with parents notified of the study through school newsletters and notices sent home to students. Youth assent for participation was obtained for all participants. Teachers were not present during data collection, which occurred during the school day.

Primary data analysis used for the testing of the study hypotheses were OLS multiple regressions. Gender, parental involvement, trait aggression, stress, family/peer support and exposure to video game violence, as well as the interaction between exposure to violent video game and trait aggression, were entered simultaneously in the regression equation. In keeping with the recommendations of Simmons et al. (2011), we certify that this analysis approach was selected in advance and was not altered to produce particular results. An interaction between trait aggression and exposure to video game violence was tested by first centering the variables to avoid multicollinearity. Collinearity diagnostics for all regressions revealed absence of any concerns with all VIFs below 2.0. Youth with depressive or attention deficit symptoms will be considered separately.

Results

Video Game Exposure

Children in our sample were generally very familiar with electronic games. Of our sample, 84.4 % reported playing video games on a computer, 81.2 % on a console and 50.4 % on a handheld device in the previous 6 months. Only 6.1 % reported playing no games at all during that time. Similarly, only 11.4 % of our sample had no exposure to violent video games. Boys had considerably more exposure to violent video games than did girls [t (189.24) = 9.07, p\

VIDEO GAMES CAN BE GOOD FOR YOU—IN MODERATION

A small study offers a mixed view on whether video games may make kids more aggressive.

Those children who spend more time playing games might be slightly likelier to be hyperactive and to get into fights. But violent video games seem to have no effect on behavior, according to British researchers.

The researchers also said they discovered that kids who played video games for less than an hour a day were more likely to be less aggressive and rated as better-behaved by their teachers.

[...] The researchers found that the 22 kids who played video games the most each day were the likeliest to have behavioral problems, exhibit hyperactivity and have trouble academically, although the effects were "quite small in magnitude," Przybylski said.

[...] The kinds of video games that the kids played appeared to have no effect after the researchers adjusted their statistics so factors such as gender wouldn't have an effect.

And there was even an unexpected benefit to playing for short amounts of time each day, the study authors found.

"Individuals who regularly played less than an hour a day of any type of game were actually less likely than their non-playing peers to fight with or bully peers and were rated as better behaved by their teachers," said study co-author Allison Fine Mishkin, a graduate student at Oxford Internet Institute. "This suggests that, in small doses, video games are a valuable and valid form of play which we do not need to fear."

"Violent Video Games Don't Influence Kids' Behavior: Study," by Randy Dotinga, Healthday, April 3, 2015.

.001, r = .46, 95 % CI = .38, .54]. Kurtosis and skew were acceptable, suggesting a normal distribution of scores.

Video Game Influences

With the sample of children with clinically elevated depressive symptoms and regarding delinquent criminality as an outcome only stress (b = .30) and trait aggression (b = .42) were predictive of delinquent criminality. Neither exposure to video game violence nor the interaction between trait aggression and exposure to video game violence were predictive of delinquent outcomes. The adjusted R2 for this regression equation was .36. With the same sample of children with clinically elevated depressive symptoms but considering bullying behaviors as an outcome, once again only stress (b = .23) and trait aggression (b = .28) were predictive of bullying behaviors. Neither exposure to video game violence nor the interaction between exposure to video game violence and trait aggression were predictive of bullying related outcomes.

[…]

Finally, with the sample once again of children with clinically elevated attention deficit symptoms and with regards to bullying behavior only trait aggression (b = .41) was predictive of bullying behaviors along with the interaction between trait aggression and exposure to violent games (b =—.22) suggesting that highly trait aggressive children who also played violent video games were less likely to engage in bullying behaviors. Exposure to video game violence was not a significant predictor of bullying behaviors. The adjusted R2 for this regression equation was .19.

Discussion

The 2011 Supreme Court (*Brown v EMA 2011*) case seemed to have briefly cooled speculation about video game violence effects on children. The tragic 2012 shooting of young children in Newtown, Connecticut by a 20-year-old male reportedly fond of playing violent video games put the issue back on the front burner (Gun Violence Prevention Task Force 2013). The consensus from the government (e.g., Gun Violence Prevention Task Force 2013) seems to have been that current research does not consistently link exposure to video game violence with aggression or societal violence, but more research is necessary to assess effects on potentially vulnerable subgroups of children. The current study is an attempt to fill that gap by considering correlational violent video game effects in a sample of youth with clinically elevated mental health symptoms. Our results did not provide support for the hypotheses that exposure to violent video games would be associated with increased delinquency or bullying behaviors in children with elevated mental health symptoms.

Our results indicated that violent video games were associated with neither delinquent criminality nor bullying behaviors in children with either clinically elevated depressive or attention deficit symptoms. Nor did we find support for the belief that trait aggression would interact with video game violence within this sample of youth. That is a particularly interesting finding given that a combination of mental health symptoms and long-term aggressive traits are common elements to attackers who carried out school shootings (US Secret Service and US Department of Education 2002). Our results cannot, of course, be generalized to mass homicides. We do note that our findings with more general forms of youth violence are similar to those of the Secret Service report, in that trait aggressiveness and stress were risk factors for negative outcomes where exposure to video game violence was not. The only exception was our finding that, for children with elevated attention deficit symptoms, trait aggression and video game violence interacted in such a way as to predict reduced bullying. This could be considered some small correlational evidence for a cathartic type effect, although we note it was for only one of four outcomes and small in effect size. Thus we caution against overinterpretation of this result.

None of the hypotheses related to video game violence effects on vulnerable youth were supported. Although this is only one piece of evidence, this early result does not support the belief that certain at-risk populations of youth, at least related to clinically elevated depression and attention deficit symptoms and trait aggression, demonstrate negative associations between violent video games and aggression related outcomes. It may be that the influence of media is simply too distal to impact children, even those with mental health symptoms. We do note that our results do not rule out motivational models of media use, wherein effects are driven by user motivations rather than automatic modeling of content. However, we found little evidence to support beliefs in reliable probabilistic models of automatic media modeling of violence in children with elevated depressive or attention deficit symptoms.

[…]

Limitations and Conclusions

As with all studies, ours has limitations that are important to consider. First, our sample includes children with mental health symptoms above clinical cut-off points on a validated screening tool, but screening results do not constitute official diagnoses of mental health disorders. Further, although we considered mental health and trait aggression, it is possible that other issues may place some children in vulnerable populations that we did not identify. Our study involves concurrent correlational data; thus, it is not possible to make causal inferences or to test the directionality of observed relationships. Reliabilities of the stress and parental involvement scales were also lower than ideal. These two scales appear to tap into a broad array of issues, which may explain this result; future researchers may wish to consider more narrowly constructed scales. Lastly, although our delinquency scale was compiled from existing well-validated scales, it would be valuable to see our results replicated using clinical outcomes such as the Child Behavior Checklist or criminological outcomes such as the Negative Life Events scale (Paternoster and Mazerolle 1994).

Our results suggest that the association between violent video games and aggression related outcomes in children, even those with clinically elevated mental health symptoms, may be minimal. Our research contributes to the field of youth and media by providing evidence that a timely, policy-relevant, and seemingly reasonable hypothesis— that mentally vulnerable children may be particularly influenced by violent video games—does not appear to be well supported. However, more research on this population, and on others likely to be at increased risk (such as children exposed to violence in their homes or neighborhoods), is needed to guide parents, health professionals and policymakers. It may be valuable for future researchers to consider alternate models of youth's media use, particularly those that focus on motivational models in which users, rather than content, drive experiences. Content-based theoretical models do not appear to be sufficient for a sophisticated understanding of media use and effects.

A Word of Caution

Scholarship produced in the emotional and politicized environment that follows a national tragedy (see Ferguson 2013) can give the appearance of a "wag the dog" effect, with research commissioned based upon, and then used to support, an a priori political agenda. As Hall et al. (2011) noted in their article on the Supreme Court and video games, a rush to judgment grounded in legislators' interpretations of "unsettled science" may damage the credibility of the scientific process. Scholars would be wise to proceed carefully, with close attention to sound methodology and discussion of limitations, as they design and conduct the next wave of studies. Studies which move beyond traditional social cognitive automatic processes to consider how youth select, interpret and involve media in their identity development as active consumers of media would be of particularly high value.

References

Brown v EMA. (2011). Retrieved July 1, 2011 from http://www. supremecourt.gov/opinions/10pdf/08-1448.pdf.

Ferguson, C. J. (2013). Violent video games and the Supreme Court: Lessons for the scientific community in the wake of Brown v EMA. American Psychologist, 68(2), 57–74.

134 J Youth Adolescence (2014) 43:127–136 123

Ferguson, C. J., & Dyck, D. (2012). Paradigm change in aggression research: The time has come to retire the General Aggression Model. Aggression and Violent Behavior, 17(3), 220–228. doi:10.1016/j.avb.2012.02.007.

Gun Violence Prevention Task Force. (2013). It's time to act: A comprehensive plan that reduces gun violence and respects the 2nd amendment rights of law-abiding Americans. Washington, DC: US House of Representatives.

Hall, R., Day, T., & Hall, R. (2011). A plea for caution: Violent video games, the Supreme Court, and the role of science. Mayo Clinic Proceedings, 86(4), 315–321.

Olweus, D. (1996). The Revised Olweus Bully/Victim Questionnaire. Mimeo. Bergen: Research Center for Health Promotion (HEMIL Center), University of Bergen.

Paternoster, R., & Mazerolle, P. (1994). General strain theory and delinquency: A replication and extension. Journal of Research in Crime and Delinquency, 31(3), 235–263.

Przybylski, A. K., Rigby, C., & Ryan, R. M. (2010). A motivational model of video game engagement. Review of General Psychology, 14(2), 154–166. doi:10.1037/a0019440.

Sherry, J. L., Lucas, K., Greenberg, B. S., & Lachlan, K. (2006). Video game uses and gratifications as predictors of use and game preference. In P. Vorderer & J. Bryant (Eds.), Playing video games: Motives, responses, and consequences (pp. 213–224). Mahwah, NJ: Lawrence Erlbaum Associates. J Youth Adolescence (2014) 43:127–136 135 123

Simmons, J. P., Nelson, L. D., & Simonsohn, U. (2011). Falsepositive psychology: Undisclosed flexibility in data collection and analysis allows presenting anything as significant. Psychological Science, 22(11), 1359–1366. doi:10.1177/09567976114 17632.

United States Secret Service and United States Department of Education. (2002). The final report and findings of the Safe School Initiative: Implications for the prevention of school attacks in the United States. Retrieved July 2, 2011 from http:// www.secretservice.gov/ ntac/ssi_final_report.pdf.

> *"Gaming violence isn't the major
> cause of real-world violence, but it
> probably is enough of a catalyst to
> warrant concern."*

We Can't Ignore the Connections Between Violent Video Games and Criminal Activity

Andy Ruddock

In the following viewpoint, Andy Ruddock looks at the big picture of the violent video game controversy and argues that, while violent video games are not the singular cause of mass shootings and other criminal activity, evidence points to a connection that should be acknowledged. It's true that all gamers aren't criminals, he says, but enough criminals have been linked to obsessive playing of video games to warrant investigation. Ruddock advises against the current binary thinking regarding video games and suggests that we instead try to get to the root of violence. Ruddock is senior lecturer at tschool of media, film, and journalism at Monash University and is the author of Youth and Media.

As you read, consider the following questions:

1. What program did Southington initiate?

2. What group blamed the gaming industry after Sandy Hook?

3. Which previous massacre was also blamed on video games?

The Connecticut town of Southington last week introduced a videogames return program, offering a $25 gift card to parents who wanted to rid their households of violent titles.

The program comes in the wake of the December 14 shootings at the Sandy Hook Elementary School in Newtown—roughly 50km south west of Southington—which claimed the lives of 20 children and six staff members.

The main aim of the "buy-back" initiative is to create a forum where the media's role in cultures of violence can be discussed. It is not an attempt to demonise games or the people who play them.

School officials recognise violence as a complicated social problem. They are aware that the media violence debate is but a strand of a much bigger conversation on the causes of the real thing.

The Southington buy-back scheme demonstrates a sophisticated understanding of the lessons of research on the effects of playing violent videogames. It finds unlikely allies within the games community, as gamers have stepped forward to consider what a love of violent videogames really means, after Newtown.

In this sense, while elements of the National Rifle Association (NRA) seek to divert attention from the role that gun ownership plays in mass murder, gamers appear more willing to grasp the JFK nettle, asking what they can do for their country.

Right after the Sandy Hook massacre, the NRA pointed an accusing finger at the videogames industry. Their position has attracted congressional support. One reaction to these developments has been to argue that studies on the effects of videogame violence on gamers are inconclusive.

They are not.

In 2010, the noted effects researcher Craig Anderson was lead author of a survey which carefully analysed the results of 130 studies on videogame violence. Anderson's findings were quite clear.

There is reliable evidence that a long-term diet of violent game playing leads to an increase in real-life aggression. The size of the effects noted in these studies were small, but statistically and socially significant.

In other words, gaming violence isn't the major cause of real-world violence, but it probably is enough of a catalyst to warrant concern. All the more so because while many things can provoke aggression—for instance, non-violent games can do the same thing if they are frustratingly difficult to play—violent videogames are designed to spark aggressive responses.

At the same time, Anderson and colleagues cautioned that the policy implications of these findings are unclear.

First, where the research addresses aggression, social anxieties are focused on physical violence. In this way, most of what we know about (aggression) doesn't directly address that which worries us most (physical violence).

Second, it may also be that videogame violence also has a range of positive effects. The problem, in this regard, is that there is a bias in effects studies toward looking for the damage games can cause among some groups.

In either case, the confident conclusion that videogame violence is bad for a significant number of people does not imply prohibition. Instead, Anderson argues that videogame violence is an environmental risk that has to be managed.

The problem, then, is that the research on videogame violence does not lend itself to quick and easy, crowd-pleasing policy action. In the resultant political vacuum, it's been interesting to see gaming insiders step up to reflect on their role in glamorising guns.

Games reviewers have challenged the industry and its consumers to take action. The games industry has been accused of playing into the hands of the NRA, by becoming over-reliant on violence as a quick and easy narrative device.

This laziness has been criticised as an abrogation of creative responsibility; a failure of games and gaming as a form of creative expression.

Perhaps the most chilling exemplar here has been the collusion between the games and gun industries, where the former has become a product placement vehicle for the latter.

Approaching gaming as an art form, games reviewers have called for the industry to take more responsibility in making the genre about expression, rather than commerce.

This mirrors the argument put forward by MIT media scholar Henry Jenkins, in the wake of the 1999 Columbine Massacre which claimed 13 lives. There, too, first-person shooter games were identified as catalysts for mass murder.

Jenkins argued against banning games, but acknowledged there were reasons to worry about the prevalence of violence in them. The trouble with most gaming violence, for Jenkins, was that it was boring.

Gamers were offered the same scenarios and options time and time again, which meant that the genre rarely fulfilled its unique capacity to make users reflect on the morality of the choices they made.

Jenkins argued that videogames could spark a productive conversation about the motivations toward violence, and the fact that they rarely did was cause for concern indeed.

This is why the positions being taken by the Southington school system and the gaming community are so smart. Reviewers who are, in the end, part of a promotional machine that popularises the gaming industry, are exploring how they can become part of the solution by embracing a position as part of the problem.

By doing so, they enable a dialogue with people who are quite legitimately concerned about violent videogames—including parents and teachers in Southington.

Together, these groups have set a leadership standard for a debate on media and violence that might actually achieve something.

Periodical and Internet Sources Bibliography

The following articles have been selected to supplement the diverse views presented in this chapter.

Dmitri Barvinok "Bullies in Video Games: Griefers," *The New Bullying,* February 15, 2012.

Michael Brown "Violent Video Games and Mass Murder," *Town Hall,* May 30, 2014.

Christopher J. Ferguson "Stop Blaming Violent Video Games," *U.S. News & World Report*, August 2, 2016.

Marybeth Hicks "Hicks: Video Games and Bullying," *Washington Times*, April 19, 2011.

William Hicks "Gaming Press Quick to Link Video Games with Orlando Shooting," *Heatstreet*, June 13, 2016.

Mike Jaccarino "Training Simulation: Mass Killers Often Share Obsession with Violent Video Games," *Fox News,* September 12, 2013.

Ryan Jaslow "Violent Video Games and Mass Violence: a Complex Link," *CBS News*, February 18, 2013.

Erik Kain "Do Games Like 'Grand Theft Auto V Cause Real-World Violence?" *Forbes*, September 8, 2013.

Ravneet Sandu "Bullying in the Gaming World," *Beyond Bullies*, Feb 1, 2015.

Susan Scutti "Do Video Games Lead to Violence?" *CNN*, July 26, 2016.

Should the Government Regulate Violent Video Games?

Chapter Preface

Government regulation, especially when it comes to the media and art, has continually served as a breeding ground of controversy. Violent video game regulation is no exception, and has been, if anything, more controversial than many other issues. Opinions range from having no regulations at all to completely banning sales of violent video games.

Banning the games has already been tested by a law passed in California in 2005 that would have fined retailers $1000 for selling violent video games to children under the age of 18. The entertainment industry and gaming industry responded to the law by taking their fight all the way to the Supreme Court. The law was ultimately overturned on the grounds that it violated the First Amendment right to free speech, and that there was not enough evidence that violent games cause psychological damage to young people.

The entertainment industry has already established some parameters in the formation of the ESRB, the Entertainment Software Ratings Board. The ratings include Early Child (EC), Everyone (E), Everyone 10+(E10), Teen (T), Mature (M), and Adults Only (AO). While retailers have agreed not to sell M or AO rated games to minors, it is a voluntary agreement and not necessarily upheld by all retailers at all times. There is no regulatory board to ensure compliance, nor do any consequences exist if the agreement is violated.

Many feel that parental supervision is the most important and ultimate regulation of violent video games and that government shouldn't take the place of parental involvement and decision making for their children. Others feel that those decisions would be unnecessary if the games were not even on the shelves or available to children under the age of 18.

On a deeper level, our society has always been violent and media is a reflection of culture. Would banning all violence from television and video games rid our culture of violence? Only if they are the cause of it. And that would be an oversimplification of an extremely complex issue. But where exactly should the line be drawn on how much media violence is too much and who decides who draws the line?

The following chapter addresses the subject of whether or not the government should have a hand in regulating the content of video games.

> "Existing policies associated with restricting the consumption of violent video games are distinct from those governing other areas where minors may be harmed psychologically. No one cohesive national policy exists."

More Studies, More Policies Needed for Video Games

Joyram Chakraborty and Nirali Chakraborty

In the following viewpoint, Joyram Chakraborty and Nirali Chakraborty address and evaluate regulations regarding the use and sale of violent video games. While a rating system already exists, the authors propose a warning system be built into the games that would make gamers aware of the consequences—both legal and psychological—of playing the games. They also note that studies regarding a causal relationship between violent video games and violent actions have not been definitive enough to generalize to the public and that more behavioral studies are needed to assist policymakers with regulatory decisions. Chakraborty is assistant professor of information systems at Towson University. Chakraborty is the research advisor at Population Services International.

As you read, consider the following questions:

1. What is the goal of this paper?
2. What two main approaches have been tried to protect minors from the effects of violent video games?
3. What is the proposed incremental solution and what is its purpose?

Public policies can influence many different types of interfaces. Popular topics within HCI [human–computer interaction] that are subject to rules and regulations include accessibility, voting, and healthcare. However, as the HCI community has gotten more involved with the development of gaming systems, it is also important to examine how games are influenced by policies aimed at protecting the greater good.

Due to the creation of gaming industry associations, a ratings system was adopted. In some U.S. states and in other countries, laws have stipulated who should have access to violent computer games, punishable by fines or incarceration. Computer gaming is also one of the rare areas of human-computer interaction where there has been a U.S. Supreme Court ruling. While that ruling upheld the First Amendment right to freedom of speech over the State of California's attempt to restrict the sale of certain games to minors, the gaming industry has voluntarily developed a code of marketing with regard to young people [1]. Our goal here is to review the literature and policies related to violence in computer gaming, provide a description of the various policy approaches that have taken place, and propose an HCI-oriented intervention to increase awareness of the relationship between violent games and aggressive behavior.

One of the earliest video games was *Pong*, released in 1972. This game was popular among arcade enthusiasts and did not include any violence. One of the first video games to incorporate aspects of violence was *Deathrace*, released in 1976. By the early 1990s, popular computing games such as *Mortal Kombat*, *Wolfenstein*, and *Street Fighter* all revolved around violence. The goals of these games were centralized around three main objectives: wounding, maiming, or killing opponents, and they featured graphics such as blood and sound effects such as screaming. At the time, players found these games to be advanced and very intriguing. Studies have indicated that by the end of the 20th century, gamer preferences for graphically enhanced violent computer games increased significantly, with easy access for players of all ages. The study of fourth graders' gaming preferences found that 59 percent of girls and 73 percent of boys preferred violent computer games [2].

From the field of public health, Sir Bradford Hill, a British physician, proposed a set of criteria by which relationships such as those seen between violent video games and violent behavior can be measured. If one were to apply these criteria (strength, consistency, specificity, temporality, dose response, plausibility, coherence, experiment, and analogy) to this relationship, one would find that approximately half of Hill's criteria are met [3]. Similarly, we could state that playing violent games is neither a necessary nor a sufficient cause of a violent outcome. Not all violence is the result of violent game play, and violent game play alone is not responsible for violence. In spite of an inability to definitively link violent video games with violent behaviors, policymakers have repeatedly examined this problem.

In the court of public opinion, excessive play of violent computer games has been blamed for mass shootings, such as the tragedies at Columbine and Newtown. Conclusive evidence demonstrating that play of violent games is causally linked to future violent behavior does not exist. However, while some meta-analytic studies have found strong relationships between video games and violence [4], others posit that violent video games are only one of several factors that combine to result in violent behavior. These other factors include genetic predisposition, family influences, and the presence of a stressful environment [5].

Existing policies associated with restricting the consumption of violent video games are distinct from those governing other areas where minors may be harmed psychologically [6]. No one cohesive national policy exists. U.S. states have asked for additional scientific evidence to demonstrate causation, notably, a 2008 Joint State Government Commission for the General Assembly of Pennsylvania's Task Force on Violent Video Games [7] and a 2013 commission established by the Commonwealth of Massachusetts [8]. This is in contrast to rules prohibiting minors from engaging in other actions that have not been conclusively linked to harmful outcomes, such as viewing pornography and purchasing lottery tickets. For these actions, policymakers found that the association alone was sufficient to take action; causality was not necessary. In other words, it did not matter if buying a lottery ticket caused direct harm, but the association between a lottery, gambling, and debt for some adults was enough to sway the government to prohibit young people from buying the tickets. In a way, lawmakers are contradicting themselves—in some instances, the association or fear of future harm is sufficient, while in others, such as for video games, a causal relationship is necessary.

To date, two main approaches to protect minors from the effects of violent video games have been tried. These differ in their strength as well as their legality in the U.S. In other arenas, however, policymakers have used additional approaches to ensure that individuals are fully aware of risks they are voluntarily engaging in.

Policies Related to Gaming and Violence: Two Approaches

Designing and implementing policy can be quite challenging, especially with rapidly evolving technology such as video games. Currently, two broad approaches are attempting to curtail the possible negative effects of violent video games: educating the consumer through the use of a video game rating system and limiting the access of minors to restricted materials.

Provide a rating system.

When possible, many public policies utilize existing industry or international standards; the regulation of violence in video games is no different. The main method of regulation adopted by most state and local governments who enact video game legislation is to defer to the Entertainment Software Ratings Board (ESRB) for age-controlled appropriateness [9]. Created in 1994, the ESRB is an industry self-regulatory group that assigns age-based labels to video games, ranging from "C" for early childhood, "E" for everyone, "T" for teen, "M" for mature, and "AO" for adults only. For example, the Matheson's Video Games Ratings Enforcement Act, H.R. 287, would make it illegal for anyone to ship, distribute, sell, or rent a video game without an age-appropriate label for the ESRB [10]. This bill was introduced in the U.S. Congress in January 2013 and has been referred to the Subcommittee on Commerce, Manufacturing, and Trade [11]. Most legislative bodies rely on retailers and parental education for the enforcement of these regulations. The sanctions for violations of the ESRB range from fines to felony convictions.

The challenges associated with video games and violence are not specific to the U.S. In the U.K., the Entertainment and Leisure Software Publishers Association (ELSPA) was formed in 1989 with the objective of bringing the content of video and computer games to the attention of the government [12]. In 1993, the Video Standards Council (VSC) was created to develop an age-restricted video game rating system [12]. The European Union (EU) created a new rating system called the Pan European Games Information (PEGI) with the objective of creating a unified rating system across the majority of the EU countries [13]. The PEGI has eight categories: age-level appropriateness, violence, bad language, fear, sex, drugs, discrimination, and gambling. It uses symbols easily understood by parents, children, and retailers.

Restrict sales.

Over the past two decades, several local and state laws have been passed to attempt to control the sale and distribution of violent video games to minors. In 2000, the city of Indianapolis attempted to enforce an ordinance that forbade any video game operator with five or more machines to allow a minor to play without the supervision of a guardian. In the same year, St. Louis County in Missouri passed an ordinance making it illegal for anyone to distribute violent video games to a minor without the consent of a guardian. In 2003, Washington State banned the sale of violent video games to minors. In 2005, the state of Illinois banned the sale or rental of violent video games to minors. In the same year, Michigan and California also passed legislation banning the sale of violent video games that had the potential to harm minors. In 2006, Oklahoma amended existing legislation for crimes against public indecency and morality to include the sale of material such as violent video games to minors. The same year, Minnesota passed the Minnesota Restricted Video Game Act, which made it illegal for a person under the age of 17 to rent or purchase age-restricted material knowingly or unknowingly. In 2007, New York passed legislation that would make the dissemination of indecent video games to minors a felony and also required equipment allowing video game console owners to prevent the display of violent video games to minors. Very little empirical work has been carried out to determine the effectiveness of these legislations.

Each attempt at enacting legislation in the U.S. has met strong opposition from gamers, industry leaders, and First Amendment advocates. Federal courts have consistently invalidated these legislative efforts to restrict minors' access to violent video games based on their content as a violation of the First Amendment. The federal appellate courts heard the constitutional arguments for 10 years before the Supreme Court ruled on the issue. In 2011, the Supreme Court decided *Brown v. Entertainment Merchants Association* by upholding a Ninth Circuit Court of Appeals decision that invalidated a California law prohibiting the sale of violent games to minors [1]. The Supreme Court and every prior federal court that has considered the issue, with only a few exceptions, have held that video games enjoy full First Amendment protection and that state efforts to regulate them must therefore survive strict scrutiny [14].

Future Direction for HCI Researchers and Practitioners

Due to the sensitive nature of violence in gaming, and due to the growth of gaming and HCI's increased involvement, it is important for our community to become aware of these issues. Video games themselves are evolving; they are no longer tied to arcades, desktops, or laptops. Devices such as smartphones and tablets are making video games ubiquitous. In addition, the effects of violent video games are not restricted to minors. Adults, who have easier access to restricted materials, are also vulnerable to the effects of these games. This will make the implementation of any future policy more challenging.

An incremental solution for HCI researchers and practitioners might be the use of informative, easy-to-read warning messages at the beginning of the video games. Similar to messages warning against video piracy used in DVDs, these messages could warn players of potential fines and felony charges for the possession of age-restricted material. These video-game-based messages could also serve as an education tool, informing players of the potential risks associated with continued long-term exposure to elements in video games such as violence. The messages could be developed using a combination of easy-to-understand symbols and words translated for the target audience. To ensure user acceptance, the messages should be developed using gamers' participation and pilot tested thoroughly with the appropriate end users to determine their effectiveness. These warning messages could be placed on the cover of the video games as well as in the game upon loading. Similar in functionality to DVD messages, this warning should display for approximately 30 seconds, and the option to skip through it should be disabled.

While this may not be the ultimate solution to the possible effects of violent video games, it does provide policymakers and HCI practioners with a low-cost, incremental solution while suitable policies are determined. The solution with the warning messages could be implemented with minimal costs to game developers. Showing the message for 30 seconds could ensure that the video gamer was made aware of the possible consequences of long-term exposure, thereby allowing them to make an educated choice.

There is a significant gap in the literature with regard to video games and violence. Very few empirical studies have been carried out to determine whether a causal relationship exists between violence in video games and individual acts of violence. Most of the reported findings draw conclusions using interviews or surveys of video gamers who have played a predetermined amount of video games. Though the findings from these studies are accurate according to the parameters of the study, they cannot be generalized to the public due to the limited sample size and the predetermined set of video games used.

The HCI community can make significant contributions to assist policymakers by understanding video gamers' behaviors and preferences toward various aspects of violent video games— for example, by studying gamers' intensity preferences for violent gaming elements such as blood or blood splatter, weapons, or style of killing. Other preferences that could potentially be determined include duration of game play and sound or haptic feedback. Using longitudinal data collection of video gamers' behaviors and preferences, it could be possible to draw conclusions about the causality of video games and violence. The findings from such studies would be of great assistance to policymakers in the implementation of carefully crafted legislation based on scientifically determined findings.

References

1. Ferguson, C.J. Violent video games and the supreme court: Lessons for the scientific community in the wake of Brown v. Entertainment Merchants Association. American Psychologist 68, 2 (2013), 57.

2. Anderson, C.A. and Bushman, B.J. Effects of violent video games on aggressive behavior, aggressive cognition, aggressive affect, physiological arousal, and prosocial behavior: A meta-analytic review of the scientific literature. Psychological science 12, 5 (2001), 353–359.

3. Hill, A.B. The environment and disease: association or causation? Proc. of the Royal Society of Medicine 58, 5 (1965), 295.

4. Anderson, C.A. An update on the effects of playing violent video games. Journal of Adolescence 27, 1 (2004), 113–122.

5. Ferguson, C.J. The school shooting/violent video game link: Causal relationship or moral panic? Journal of Investigative Psychology and Offender Profiling 5, 1–2 (2008), 25–37.

6. McCollum, B.J. Violent Video Games and Symptoms of Distress and Trauma. Thesis. Georgia Southern University, 2014.

7. Committee, A. Comprehensive analysis of violent crime and mass shootings. 2013; http://jsg.legis.state.pa.us/resources/documents/ftp/publications/2013-365-VPAC%20 Report%201.1.14.pdf

8. Brownsberger, W.N., Hecht, J., and Lawn, J.J. Commission to investigate video games as a form of media and as a training tool. 2013.

9. Chang, J. Rated M for mature: Violent video game legislation and the obscenity standard. Journal of Civil Rights and Economic Development 24, 4 (2012), 3.

10. Sasso, B. and Kasperowicz., P. Dem lawmaker introduces bill to ban sales of violent video games to minors. The Hill. Jan. 17, 2013; http://thehill.com/policy/ technology/277781-dem-bill-would-ban-sale-of-violent-games-to-minors

11. Matheson, J. Video Games Ratings Enforcement Act, 2013.

12. Barlett, C.P. and Anderson, C. Violent video games and public policy. In Wie wir spielen, was wir werden: Computerspiele in unserer Gesellschaft. T. Bevc and H. Zapf, ed. UVK Verlagsgesellschaft, Konstanz, 2009.

13. Pan European Game Information; http://www.pegi.info/en/index

14. Dunkelberger, J. The new Resident Evil? State regulation of violent video games and the First Amendment. BYU Law Review (2011), 1659.

> "While [video games] can help to teach math and science, they can also help teach sociopathic behaviors. And those behaviors are the ones that need to be nipped in the bud, and this can only be accomplished by pulling those violent games off the shelves."

Violent Video Games Should Be Banned

Eric Roberts

In the following viewpoint, Eric Roberts argues that violent video games should be pulled off the shelves because of the deleterious effects that they have on children. Some of these effects include loss of empathy, sexism, increased violence, and addictive behavior. While the author admits that art and free expression are important, and that some video games are beneficial, he asserts that ultra-violent video games should be banned. Roberts is a regular contributor to DiscussMuch magazine.

As you read, consider the following questions:

1. What does the author consider to be the worst effect of violent video games?
2. How does the author feel about the way women are portrayed in violent games and what effect on game players does this have?
3. List some of the other effects that the author feels violent games have on children.

Violent Video Games Produce Violent Behavior

Human beings have never really been peace-loving people. For as far back as history can be traced, there have been wars and needless killings and senseless violence. However, never before in human history have we bottled these things up to use as entertainment. With today's graphically intense video game machines, we have made war, rape, murder and violence an everyday thing that nobody bats an eye over, and it's wreaking havoc on the psyches of our children. Violent video games equate to violent behavior, especially in children whose brains are not fully formed yet, and they need to be stopped.

Sure, a ratings system on video games is a good thing to have, but if we're being honest about it, a game rated MA (Mature) doesn't stop a kid from playing it. It just stops a kid from buying it. Those games are still out there and readily available for children, and they're doing harm in ways that most people cannot even imagine.

Why Violent Video Games Need to be Banned from Store Shelves

Let's deal with the worst first, because that's most important. Kids playing violent video games are completely losing their empathy. They're being programmed to only experience joyful sensations associated with violence. They get their kicks from blowing someone's head off in *Grand Theft Auto*, and they're numb outside of that sensation. So, like a drug addict chasing a high, these

ENFORCING CONTENT RATINGS

[...] If you have either purchased a video game or seen one advertised on TV, you know that games are age-rated, much like movies are. The industry should be applauded for having one of the most robust content-rating standards of all the various types of media. The problem lies in the retail sales. In recent "secret shopper" efforts, grassroots members of the Parents Television Council demonstrated that an underage child was able to purchase an adult video game 36 percent of the time. The U.S. Federal Trade Commission conducted similar "secret shopper" investigations and found still-disappointing failure rates, in the range of 20 percent.

"The Government Should Stop Kids From Buying Violent Video Games," by Timothy Winter, U.S. News & World Report, May 10, 2010.

children develop violent tendencies in order to create that feeling in the real world. This is a contributing factor to school shootings being on the rise, as well as teenage sex and rape, and drug use, and violence in general. It all has its roots in violent video games. Now, nobody's saying kids were perfect angels before video games came along. We all know that's not true. However, since violent video games have became popular, we've seen children committing more dangerous and violent behaviors. The correlation is so tight that to ignore the causation is to be willfully blind.

Not only are violent video games producing more violent youngsters, but the impact is more far-reaching than most can truly imagine. For example, let's look at the way women are treated in video games. Women fall into one of a few categories. They're either helpless victims, disposable background decorations, or sexual objects for male fantasies. This is how women are portrayed in games. You can beat and murder them with impunity. You can have your way with them. They are helpless to help themselves. And they're thrown into video games to be fodder for male urges. This leads to young males developing sexist attitudes towards women, and this is something that can damage society for generations.

If the violence isn't bad enough, a generation of men growing up to view women as meaningless background decoration and fantasy fodder for the male libido is a vast amount of damage that cannot be easily cleaned up.

The Side Effects of Violent Video Games

Some of you reading this might believe that things are being overblown here and that violent video games really don't have these dire consequences. However, you're missing the forest for the trees. Yes, art is important; free expression is important. Video games do have a place in our society. But the ultra-violent video games are little more than training tools for young people, teaching them how to be violent. Violent video games can cause a lot of damage to younger people, including but not limited to:

- Children who play violent video games stimulate their brains with violence and thus seek to recreate that stimulation
- Empathy is lost more readily in children who play violent video games
- Violent video games teach children that nothing is to be valued in life save their own selfish desires
- Children learn how to use weapons and how to fight in the most crude, violent ways imaginable
- The true-to-life graphics take gaming today out of the fantasy realm and put violence into the real world
- Video games can teach young boys to grow up disrespecting women and treating them as sexual objects
- Violent games can create an addict out of youngsters, leaving them chasing that "high" associated with committing violence

Listed above are just a few of the many, many negative side effects associated with violent video games. We don't want to create any confusion here. We are not in any way against video games. Video games can be tremendously engaging and effective teaching tools. But that knife cuts both ways, for lack of a better analogy. While they can help to teach math and science, they can also help teach sociopathic behaviors. And those behaviors are the ones that need to be nipped in the bud, and this can only be accomplished by pulling those violent games off the shelves.

| "*Overall, the responsibility of regulating content is an issue best left to the industry and its community."*

Do We Need More Video Game Violence Regulation?

Shawn Schuster

In the following viewpoint, Shawn Schuster curates various viewpoints from knowledgable bloggers about government regulation for video games. The majority of opinions fall on the side of little or no government regulations for various reasons. While most agree that some regulation is necessary, they feel that job should fall to the entertainment industry, the retail industry, and parents of minors, not the government. Schuster is a games journalist and former managing editor of Massively, a gaming blog that closed in January 2015.

As you read, consider the following questions:

1. Why does one blogger feel that ratings are important?
2. At what should game developers take a hard look?
3. Where do most of the bloggers feel the responsibility for regulating game content should lie and why?

"The Think Tank: Should the Government Regulate Bideo Game Content?" by Shawn Schuster, The Atlantic Monthly Group, January 24, 2013. Reprinted by permission.

While government regulation is welcomed in some corners of our lives, it's not always welcomed everywhere. After recent gun violence has been making headlines more than ever, U.S. President Barack Obama set out to "find the cause" through new funding for 23 executive orders that pertain to the origins of gun violence. Vice President Joe Biden then met with experts in the video game industry to discuss the possibility that video games themselves are the cause. And probably that rock 'n' roll music, too. Darn kids!

Certainly we here at Massively have our own opinion on this matter, as video game violence legislation would affect us all. Read on past the cut to see what we have to say about government regulation for our favorite hobby.

Beau

Over the years, the government—state or federal—has stepped in to clarify what a citizen can and cannot do. The government puts controls on our "freedom" all the time. In my state, Texas, you have to have a minimum level of insurance on your car. In my city, it is now illegal to smoke while in a diner. Contrary to internet slacktivism, we do not have absolute free speech. The government exists in many ways to control or enforce laws on the people. And no, I am not comparing doing without car insurance to viewing violent gameplay.

I cannot say that in every case it should be legal to allow a child to play a video game. Ask me in 20 years when virtual reality allows photorealistic, bloody gameplay and sexual encounters. The fact is that we will have to morph our views depending on the technology. I think that video game sales should be treated like pornography, meaning that we should have agreed, law-enforced limits to the material. At a certain point humans of a certain, agreed-upon age cannot take part. As with most issues like this, it's an argument over where the lines should be drawn, not if they should be drawn. That argument is nowhere near over.

Bree

This one's just too easy an answer: No, not in the least. I don't want to see governments meddling in any sort of art or entertainment at all. So tired of nanny states. Adults are perfectly capable of determining what they and their children should and should not be watching, reading, hearing, and playing.

David

In Australia, we have a serious problem with our government regulating video games. We have had two different GTA games banned completely, I had to show my drivers license to purchase *Age of Conan* (which was promptly removed from shelves here for about two months after release anyway), and we received an edited version of *The Witcher* for sale in Australia. So I fight for my rights to purchase and see games in their full without the government stepping in and ruining it.

With all that said, ratings are important. The reason they are important is exactly why we do not need our government to censor or regulate game content. It should be up to us, or if you are a minor, your parents, as to what you are allowed to play and see or not. Put a bigger ratings sticker on the game. Tell video game retailers to make sure the person purchasing the game can see and understand what the rating system means. Don't cut out my ability to see the content in its full, which was created as a piece of art. And that is what it is: art.

Eliot

I think we should establish a board of intelligent and experienced people to review content and provide ratings so that a reasonable choice can be made about the content of a game prior to its purchase.

Wait, that already exists? And has for nearly two decades? Wow, that was fast.

The problem isn't that the government doesn't regulate what's in video games, even disregarding the fact that video games have been found to qualify as protected speech by the Supreme Court. The problem is that there is a sizable portion of the parental population that seems to think that the ESRB rating that's appeared on the front of pretty much every game available at retailers is not actually a thing. These are parents who don't do the minimum necessary research to understand that their child should not be playing *Grand Theft Auto IV* at age eight. But it's not for lack of trying on the part of developers or the industry, just a lack of acknowledgement by the people making the purchasing decisions.

You can't legislate awareness, sadly.

Jef

No, you can't legislate personal responsibility. Even if you could, a group of self-absorbed folk who don't see the wisdom in spending less than you make would be the wrong ones to attempt it.

Justin

Yes! Absolutely! Wait... is this... a loaded question? Gasp!

Actually, I think the world would be a lot better if the government would regulate entertainment a little less and important stuff a little more. Entertainment is an expression of free speech, and I'm pretty strong about that being shielded from politicians who think that they know better than parents as to what people should and shouldn't be exposed to. The video game industry has been pretty successful at regulating itself for quite some time now, and I see no reason to change that.

That said, I do think that gamers have this incredible reflex to reject any notion that games can have a negative influence on people, and sometimes that reflex heads off what could be interesting and potentially useful discussions about the topics of addiction, violence, sexism, and so on. We are influenced by our environment, and when we choose to make that environment video games, we should always be examining what these games and the gaming culture is possibly doing to our development, habits, and growth.

Larry

Personally, I have nothing against the government giving us the tools to self-regulate. For instance, if MSRB or PEGI didn't exist, I would be pushing for some sort of national labeling on video games.

As a father of young gamers, I believe it's important for me to know about the content my kids are playing. Unfortunately, I cannot monitor every single thing they play unless I'm playing the exact same things they are all the time. That just isn't possible. Fortunately, the creators of video games took it upon themselves to give parents the tools to regulate their children's input without having to watch over the kid's shoulders. We as parents just need to be more aware of what already exists so that our children do not get exposed to the things we consider unacceptable.

The bottom line is that if the government were to step in and regulate further, then the system we have in place would get watered down and ineffectual. That said, if the government wanted to help promote safe content for children, then I would be all for it.

Mike

On the one hand, it is the government's job to enforce standards that dictate what content is and isn't available in media, so there's an argument to be made for it stepping in to monitor game content. On the other hand, the U.S. government has shown itself to be so incredibly inept at effectively regulating any industry that one has to wonder as to what they'd hope to accomplish by stepping in on the creative process behind games. Surely we'd just end up with some sort of cap-and-trade fiasco with carbon allowances replaced by side-boob and exploding heads.

Overall, the responsibility of regulating content is an issue best left to the industry and its community. The ESRB has done a fine job of rating content, and the large majority of stores uphold their recommendations. Parents should handle the other half since they're the ones with buying power, and it's on them to make sure their kids are sticking with age-appropriate content. Finally (and most importantly), developers need to take a hard look at why so many games depend on gratuitous violence and the fetishization of women and sex in lieu of mature, compelling narratives with characters worth knowing.

Patrick

I guess to answer this question, we'd have to define regulation. Ultimately my answer is dependent on the type of enforcement. Regulation similar to the motion picture industry—where kids can't buy porn and there are ID checks at R-rated movies—is OK in my book. The thing is that we already self-regulate in this manner. I would actually like to see outlets penalized for selling M-rated games to minors, so some regulation would probably be good. More heavy-handed regulation, similar to that of alcohol, tobacco, and firearms... that's pretty awful. I would definitely protest those kinds of laws.

Ultimately, as the other writers have said, the burden of good parenting isn't on the government, and no amount of regulation can ensure that our children are exposed to the right influences at the right time.

Shawn

I'm so much against this idea that I even hate talking about it on a gaming website, but this issue has been forced upon us lately, so here we are.

I think the government should only regulate rights and needs, not entertainment. That said, the president is barking up the wrong tree—or at least the wrong part of the tree. We have to figure out some way to get parents to raise their children with ideals and morals again. If you don't want your child exposed to the violence in an M-rated video game, don't buy it for them because they cry about it. Children need guidance and rules, and when you let them make adult decisions, the pressure of unexpected consequences will break them. That's usually when you find them shooting up a school for attention.

Terilynn

Wait, isn't the big thing now for people to scream, "Less government! Less government?!" Paraphrasing a quote from Dr. Bones McCoy in The Voyage Home: "The bureaucratic mentality is the only constant in the universe."

What happens if legislation does pass? Then people who think they're important and know better than you (and have scratched politicians' derrieres long enough) will be selected to be on the "blue ribbon" panel to define just what it is that will be considered "too violent" or "too suggestive." And they get to make a whole bunch of money sitting "listening" to lobbyists from every known special interest group willing to "make their point heard" just a little bit louder than another lobbyist.

Once all is said and done, after the self-righteous blue-ribbon panel members have postponed their "report" for a couple of years (because there were so many lobbyists that needed "listening to"), they'll finally get around to making their recommendations that will inevitably be a complete waste of time and millions upon millions of dollars, when really, parents should just read the labels of their kids' video games as carefully as they consider the gluten content of their cereal. So yeah. I don't really support wasting gargantuan amounts of money to produce completely useless and burdensome laws when we're all just better off taking responsibility for ourselves.

> *"Even where the protection of children
> is the object, the constitutional limits
> on governmental action apply"*

Law Banning Sales of Violent Video Games to Minors Overturned by Supreme Court

Derek Green

In the following viewpoint, Derek Green relates the reasoning and impact behind the 2011 Supreme Court decision in the case of Brown v. the Entertainment Merchants Association *that overturned a California law that would have prohibited the sale of violent video games to minors. The decision was based on its violation of First Amendment Rights. Mr. Green also addresses the views of the dissenting justices and the relevance of this Supreme Court decision to the news media. Green is a commercial and media litigation attorney and McCormick Legal Fellow of the Reporters Committee for Freedom of the Press.*

As you read, consider the following questions:

1. What did the California law do that the Court considered "unprecedented and mistaken?"
2. What were the reasons given by the dissenting justices for their votes?
3. How does this decision relate to the news media?

"Regulation of violent video games sales to minors violates First Amendment," by Derek Green, Reporters Committee for Freedom of the Press, Summer 2011. Reprinted by permission.

O n the final day of its term, the U.S. Supreme Court rejected an attempt to carve out another category of speech from First Amendment protection, striking down a California restriction on the sale or rental of violent video games to minors.

"We have no business passing judgment on the view of the California Legislature that violent video games (or, for that matter, any other forms of speech) corrupt the young or harm their moral development," Justice Antonin Scalia said for the Court. However, "[e]ven where the protection of children is the object, the constitutional limits on governmental action apply," Scalia cautioned.

Calling California's attempt to identify a new category of permissible speech regulations for violent speech directed at children "unprecedented and mistaken," the Court ruled the state law unconstitutional.

California law restricted minors' access to violent video games

The case, *Brown* (formerly *Schwarzenegger*) *v. Entertainment Merchants Association*, arose out of a challenge to the constitutionality of a California law enacted in 2005 that prohibited the sale or rental of "violent video game[s]" to minors. The law contained a detailed definition of such games, applying to those "in which the range of options available to a player includes killing, maiming, dismembering, or sexually assaulting an image of a human being" if the games also met other criteria reflecting a lack of positive value to minors.

The law also included a labeling requirement on the games, requiring violent video games to be designated as such by including a specific "18" label on the front cover.

Before the law could go into effect, the Video Software Dealers Association and the Entertainment Merchants Association challenged it in federal court. A U.S. District judge in California granted the trade groups' request to enjoin enforcement of the law, concluding that the prohibition on sales and rentals to minors violated the First Amendment. The U.S. Court of Appeals in San Francisco (9th Cir.) affirmed the ruling. The Ninth Circuit also concluded that the labeling requirement was itself unconstitutional because it impermissibly compelled the video game retailers to include a controversial message on the product that was not purely factual.

The U.S. Supreme Court agreed to review the Ninth Circuit's opinion last year. The case attracted significant attention from the media and legal communities. Interested parties filed more than 30 friend-of-the-court briefs, including one filed by the Reporters Committee for Freedom of the Press on behalf of several news media organizations.

The Reporters Committee's brief argued that the legislative reaction to violence in video games followed a long pattern of attempts to censor new forms of media, from comic books to motion pictures to rock 'n' roll music, and did not justify creating an additional exception to the First Amendment rights.

The Court heard oral arguments in the case last November, but did not issue an opinion until the final day of its term, in late June.

A "wholly new category of content-based regulation"

Scalia, writing for a five member majority, framed the case as one of content-based regulation of speech. Scalia said California "wishes to create a wholly new category of content-based regulation that is permissible only for speech directed at children."

Such a regulatory regime cannot withstand constitutional review, Scalia said. "No doubt a State possesses legitimate power to protect children from harm, but that does not include a free-floating power to restrict the ideas to which children may be exposed," Scalia said, citing past cases.

Driving home the relevance of the California law to more general principles of free speech, Scalia emphasized the difficulty in limiting First Amendment protections to certain content or topics. "The Free Speech Clause exists principally to protect discourse on public matters, but we have long recognized that it is difficult to

SACRED AND INVIOLATE RIGHTS

[…] The (video game) industry also has an independent rating system, similar to the movie rating system, that informs and empowers parents. Watchdog groups and government agencies, like the Federal Trade Commission, praise it as a system that works. A 2009 study by the FTC found that 87 percent of parents were satisfied with the computer and video game ratings. Last year, the FTC said the computer and video game industry "outpaces" other entertainment industries in restricting marketing of mature-rated products to children, clearly and prominently displaying rating information and restricting children's access to mature-rated products.

Retailers are supportive of the ratings system and are playing a critical role in keeping mature-themed video games out of the wrong hands. Virtually all major U.S. retailers are working to help parents keep control of the games children play by enforcing age restrictions.

As a medium, computer and video games are entitled to the same protections as the best of literature, music, movies, and art. In the end, Americans' rights to speech and expression are sacred and inviolate—and millions across the political spectrum agree with us.

"Video Games Don't Cause Children to be Violent," Michael D. Gallagher, U.S. News & World Report, May 10, 2010.

distinguish politics from entertainment, and dangerous to try," Scalia said.

Scalia's opinion also looked to a long history of violent content in expressive works aimed at children.

"Grimm's Fairy Tales, for example, are grim indeed," Scalia said. "As her just desserts for trying to poison Snow White, the wicked queen is made to dance in red hot slippers 'till she fell dead on the floor, a sad example of envy and jealousy.' Cinderella's evil stepsisters have their eyes pecked out by doves. And Hansel and Gretel (children!) kill their captor by baking her in an oven."

After determining that the content regulated by the California law was protected speech, the Court turned to analyzing whether such regulations were nonetheless permissible.

Justifying such content-based regulations is an uphill challenge, as such restrictions are considered constitutionally suspect and require demonstrating a "high degree of necessity [the Court has] described as a compelling state interest," Scalia said. California's law failed such scrutiny because the state had not demonstrated that the law as written would satisfy a compelling state interest and the law was not sufficiently narrowly drawn.

"As a means of protecting children from portrayals of violence, the legislation is seriously underinclusive, not only because it excludes portrayals other than video games, but also because it permits a parental or avuncular veto," Scalia said.

"And as a means of assisting concerned parents it is seriously overinclusive because it abridges the First Amendment rights of young people whose parents (and aunts and uncles) think violent video games are a harmless pastime. And the overbreadth in achieving one goal is not cured by the underbreadth in achieving the other."

The Court's opinion follows last year's decision in *United States v. Stevens*, which struck down a law prohibiting the sale of certain depictions of cruelty to animals. In Stevens, the Court warned against attempts to designate additional topics of speech as not subject to First Amendment protections. The Court reiterated that position here.

"Last Term, in Stevens, we held that new categories of unprotected speech may not be added to the list by a legislature that concludes certain speech is too harmful to be tolerated." That understanding compelled the Court to reject California's attempt to regulate violent content to minors, Scalia said.

Differing opinions

Scalia's opinion for the Court commanded only a five-justice majority. Justice Samuel Alito, writing for himself and Chief Justice John Roberts Jr., agreed that the law as written was unconstitutional. But Alito said the Court should have decided the case on vagueness grounds only.

Alito "question[ed] the wisdom of the Court's approach" in striking down the law on broader grounds and said the Court should not have embraced strict scrutiny analysis. He predicted that the effect of such a "sweeping" opinion would be to unnecessarily limit legislative efforts to combat concerns that new technologies are harmful to minors.

"I would not squelch legislative efforts to deal with what is perceived by some to be a significant and developing social problem. If differently framed statutes are enacted by the States or by the Federal Government, we can consider the constitutionality of those laws when cases challenging them are presented to us."

Alito also questioned the Court's conclusion that video games are the equivalent of books and literature for First Amendment purposes.

"When all of the characteristics of video games are taken into account, there is certainly a reasonable basis for thinking that the experience of playing a video game may be quite different from the experience of reading a book, listening to a radio broadcast, or viewing a movie. And if this is so, then for at least some minors, the effects of playing violent video games may also be quite different," Alito said. "The Court acts prematurely in dismissing this possibility out of hand."

Justices Stephen Breyer and Clarence Thomas wrote individual dissents. Thomas maintained that speech to minors is "excluded" from the First Amendment's speech protections, based on a historical understanding of the constitutional amendment.

"The practices and beliefs of the founding generation establish that 'the freedom of speech,' as originally understood, does not include a right to speak to minors (or a right of minors to access speech) without going through the minors' parents or guardians," Thomas said.

Breyer viewed the California law as facially valid. He said the law was no more vague than laws regulating sexual content in expressive materials that the Court had upheld in previous cases. Moreover, although he agreed with the Court majority that the law should be subjected to strict scrutiny review, Breyer said the law could pass such analysis.

California's Legislature passed a law to combat a societal concern about the effects of violent video games on minors and created a regulation that addressed that concern in a permissible manner, he said.

"Our Constitution cannot succeed in securing the liberties it seeks to protect unless we can raise future generations committed cooperatively to making our system of government work," Breyer said. "In my view, the First Amendment does not disable government from helping parents make . . . a choice not to have their children buy extremely violent, interactive video games, which they more than reasonably fear pose only the risk of harm to those children."

The relevance to the news media

Paul Smith, the attorney who argued the case for the video game industry, said that the Court's decision "strongly reinforced the principle that the Court is not going to create new exceptions to the First Amendment or particular types of controversial content."

Addressing the relevance of the case to the news media, Smith said: "I don't know how many times a newspaper article would be so violent that it would have fallen within some exception if [the Court had] created it, but certainly the Court's overall strong reinforcement of the notion that there are some exceptions, but we are not creating any new ones, is important."

However, Smith suggested the Court's emphasis on historical context in defining the First Amendment protections may give some press advocates pause. The defamation protections that the Supreme Court has afforded to the press, for example, may lack the historical background of other rights.

"If you wanted to take a completely originalist view then you could say that *New York Times v. Sullivan* was kind of created out of whole cloth 150 years later," Smith said. "So if you wanted to, you could take apart the whole edifice of the Sullivan line of cases to protect the press in defamation [cases]."

Smith said that he does not have a particular reason to believe that Scalia is intent on re-examining the Sullivan line of cases. Nonetheless, "it is true that an originalist view, while helpful in the violence area, would be less helpful I suppose in a defamation case, because, for a long, long time before Sullivan, states were free to punish defamation based on showings a lot less difficult than they have to show now," Smith said.

Assessing the Court's views on press freedoms based on recent speech cases remains a challenge, Smith said. "This is a strongly pro-First Amendment Court," he said. "Whether they are a strong pro-press rights Court I don't know. We haven't had a lot of press rights cases recently."

> *"The question we should be asking is not whether* Call of Duty, *or* Dexter, *or the* Saw *films are going to turn us into a nation of multi-ethnic, multi-gender, multi-generational psychopaths [...] Rather, it's why so many of us [...] feel so drawn to violent fantasies in our culture."*

Banning Violent Video Games Won't Eliminate the Violence in Our Culture

Alyssa Rosenberg

In the following viewpoint, Alyssa Rosenberg addresses the violence that is part of our culture, and why we should not be blaming violent video games or other media violence. The author feels that violence in popular culture is a reflection of real-world violence and our fears about "justice, disempowerment, and the state of civil society." She goes on to argue that narrative stories in popular culture "help us manage our reactions to the prospect of encountering that violence" which, thanks to television, we have almost come to expect. Rosenberg is a culture blogger for the Washington Post, *and has been the culture editor at* ThinkProgress, *a correspondent for* The Atlantic. com, *and a columnist for the XX Factor at* Slate.

"Why Banning Violent Video Games Won't Address Our Culture of Violence," by Alyssa Rosenberg, ThinkProgress, December 17, 2012. Reprinted by permission.

As you read, consider the following questions:

1. What does the author think we are dodging by blaming violent video games for causing violence in the real world?
2. What permeates our current culture?
3. Explain what the author means when she says that our culture believes that "escalation is the appropriate response to profound failures of justice and the social compact."

After Adam Lanza shot twenty young children and six of the teachers and administrators who helped educate them in Newtown, Connecticut on Friday, the massacre renewed the long-dormant national debate about gun control, and sparked a complementary—and in some cases diversionary—discussion about mental health funding and treatment. But it's also revived another old conversation, about whether video games are too violent, and whether they play a role in encouraging, desensitizing, and even preparing mass killers for their rampages.

Sen. Joe Lieberman, the outgoing independent from Connecticut who has long crusaded against video game manufacturers, said in his appearance on Fox News Sunday that "The violence in the entertainment culture—particularly, with the extraordinary realism to video games, movies now, et cetera—does cause vulnerable young men to be more violent...Doesn't make everybody more violent, but it's a causative factor in some cases." Obama senior strategist David Axelrod tweeted "In NFL post-game: an ad for shoot 'em up video game. All for curbing weapons of war. But shouldn't we also quit marketing murder as a game?"

As Annalee Newitz reminds us in a valuable post at io9, there is no conclusive evidence that consuming violent games, movies, or comics leads to violent behavior in the real world. And at the *Washington Post*, Max Fischer ran the numbers on video game popularity in countries with much lower rates of gun violence, and found no correlation between game play and real-world violence.

And there's something deeply sophistic, in the absence of that evidence, about pivoting away from questions of effective gun control to proposals for video game regulation or condemnation. At least discussion of the mental health care system is part of a reasonable tapestry of efforts, including gun control, that we ought to be considering, if not a substitute for conversations about magazine capacities and the reinstatement of the assault weapons ban. Blaming video games or any other kind of violent media for causing violence in the real world is a dodge from policy solutions. And it's a dodge from the conversation we actually need to have about the state of our popular culture, and the profound fears about justice, disempowerment, and the state of civil society that are reflected in it. Video games are easy to target. The things that actually, truly frighten us are much harder.

One of the things I've been turning over in my mind in recent weeks is why the renaissance in our television is so specifically concerned with, as NPR's Linda Holmes put it, "avoiding being violently killed" to the exclusion of other concerns like finding a satisfying place in the adult world, a loving, complimentary partner, doing good, honorable work, or being a good citizen in difficult circumstances. But as much as I feel somewhat burned out by the gouts of violence on my television, it's true that questions about deploying violence, avoiding it, and its moral and immoral applications, permeate our political culture and lived experience today.

If you're a woman in the United States, you're taught from a young age that you have to be careful to avoid having sexual violence visited upon you. I cannot imagine being African-American and considering how to speak to my child about the possibility that his or her interactions with law enforcement may become deadly, or that in some areas of the country, people may feel entitled to shoot them dead on slight, and imagined, provocation. There are people in this country for whom the best way to pay for college is to enlist to be sent to a protracted war that carries with it a considerable risk that they will return maimed or brain injured. We are waging a war from the skies in which our political leadership appears to accept the deaths of children as a reasonable level of collateral damage, and where 17 percent of the pilots who actually have to carry out our drone strikes are considered "clinically distressed" by their work. As many commentators have usefully pointed out, the massacre in Newtown is deeply disturbing in part because the community was not afflicted by a constant blight of gun violence like the one that spread like rot over Chicago this summer. We've lived through a political election in which obvious references to the lynching of the first black president were excused away as jokes.

There are narrative reasons for our popular culture to portray violence. But it's also possible that our popular culture is violent precisely because our larger culture is violent—though it's important to note certain kinds of crime are decreasing, it's clear we still feel overpowering levels of anxiety about even the levels that we've reached—and we need stories to help us manage our reactions to the prospect of encountering that violence.

When we live in a country where there is a backlog of 400,000 untested rape kits, and where victims of rape and sexual abuse are routinely shamed, exposed, and disbelieved, no wonder fantasies of revenge against rapists who will never be brought to true justice bloom like evil flowers in television shows like *Dexter*. The shooting deaths of Trayvon Martin and Jordan Davis by men who claimed their rights to fire were covered under so-called Stand Your Ground laws are a reminder that racialized violence of the sort depicted in Quentin Tarantino's *Django Unchained*, about a slave who vows to free his wife from a brutal plantation owner, is not so far away, and that its roots have not been fully excised from the American garden. Even though Osama bin Laden is dead, the damage he and his warped ideology did is irreversible, and popular culture will continue to give us outlets to fantasize about destroying him over and over again, from Abu Nazir's burial at sea in the season finale of *Homeland* last night to the procedural exploration of his death in *Zero Dark Thirty*.

Embedded in both our conversations about real violence and in our pop cultural responses to violence is the idea that escalation is the appropriate response to profound failures of justice and the social compact. Women should defend themselves more effectively against their abusers, or in general claim equality by appropriating violent power previously reserved for men for their own, whether they're buying blinged-out rifles or transforming themselves into kick-ass action heroines. Men should reclaim their masculinity, threatened by the economy, by feminism, or whichever culprit is popular at the moment by burrowing in, whether by adopting steroid regimens while still teenagers or purchasing the Bushmaster A-15, the gun Adam Lanza used in Connecticut, which the company that manufactures it once advertised with the slogan "Consider Your Man Card Reissued." This sort of sentiment is perfectly encapsulated by the very clever ads for the *Call of Duty* lines of video games, which carry the tagline "There's A Soldier In All Of Us," emphasizing that the slogan applies everyone from professional women of color to white fast food workers.

Writing about the real-world application of this kind of escalation, the idea that more guns, like the five that Nancy Lanza owned, make us safer at *The American Conservative*, Alan Jacobs issues a powerful reminder of what it really means: "It gives up on the rule of law in favor of a Hobbesian 'war of every man against every man' in which we no longer have genuine neighbors, only potential enemies. You may trust your neighbor for now—but you have high-powered recourse if he ever acts wrongly." Or if you believe yourself to be aggrieved by women, as Seung-Hui Cho seemed to be, or that a Congresswoman from Arizona is part of a conspiracy to manipulate American currency, as Jared Lee Loughner appeared to believe. Guns didn't save those men from the fevered fantasies of their invention. And video games didn't move them to action.

The question we should be asking is not whether *Call of Duty*, or *Dexter*, or the *Saw* films are going to turn us into a nation of multi-ethnic, multi-gender, multi-generational psychopaths, unable to or disinterested in distinguishing reality from the images we see on all kinds of screens. Violent culture has existed for years, and yet, the murderers in the mass shootings that appear to be descending on us at an escalating rate, are overwhelmingly white and overwhelmingly male. Rather, it's why so many of us, even those who will never put a rifle stock to our shoulders or wrap our hands around a pistol grip, feel so drawn to violent fantasies in our culture. Pretending that such an attraction came to life somewhere in a massively multiplayer online game is self-deluding. And acting as if shutting down the production of violent images would curb our fears and desires to fight back against them is an attempt to avoid confronting how frightening our society is for so many citizens even on ordinary days.

Periodical and Internet Sources Bibliography

The following articles have been selected to supplement the diverse views presented in this chapter.

Neils Clark "Video Game Regulation: Where We Are Now," *Gamasutra,* January 20, 2009.

Louise Egan "Video Game Content Ratings: Does Anyone Care Anymore?" *The Artifice,* January 9, 2014.

John Hudson "Regulating Violent Video Games: A Job for Parents or Government?" *The Atlantic,* April 27, 2010.

Erik Kain "Chris Christie is Right about Parents and Violent Video Games—But His Policy is Wrong," *Mother Jones,* April 25, 2013.

Adam Liptak "Justices Reject Ban on Violent Video Games for Children," *New York Times,* June 27, 2011.

Bill Mears "California ban on sale of violent video games to children rejected, *CNN,* June 27, 2011.

Giuliano Millan "Do Video Game Worlds Need Government Regulation?" *Mises Institute,* January 15, 2016.

Heather Newman "Bad News for Underage Buyers: ESRB Ratings Checks At an All-Time High," *VB,* September 16, 2014.

Kyle Orland "20 Years, 20 Questionable Game Ratings: A Timeline of ESRB Oddities," *ARS Technica,* September 16, 2014.

Keezy Young "T is for Teen: An Easy Guide to the ESRB Ratings," Pixelkin, October 28, 2013.

For Further Discussion

Chapter 1

1. In his article on the harmful effects of violent video games, Dr. Brad Bushman argues that people are in denial that violent games have any effect on them in part due to the influence of non-expert journalists who claim that they are not harmful. Do you agree or disagree with the four reasons he gives for this denial? Why or why not?

2. Lecturer Michael Kasumovic makes a case for examining not only other triggers that can cause aggression besides violent video games, but also taking into consideration our physiological makeup and natural responses to stimuli that might result in aggression. Do you find his arguments valid or inconclusive? Why or why not?

3. Matt Terzi points out that video games are an art form and that they are played for fun and even taught him to hate the evils of torture. Evaluate his stance based on his evidence and reasoning.

Chapter 2

1. The psychologists who conducted the Iowa State University studies on whether or not violent video games desensitize players to violence claim that the entertainment media's marketing system is an "effective systematic violence desensitization tool." Do you believe they make a valid case for this? Why or why not?

2. Brad J. Bushman and Christopher Ferguson take different views of whether or not violent video games desensitize gamers. With whom do you agree, if either, and why?

3. In their study, Hasan, Begue and Bushman measured cardiac coherence levels to determine that playing

violent video games causes stress, which makes people more aggressive. Do you think the three limitations they mentioned (only measuring one type of aggressive behavior, using a large percentage of females in the study, and excluding other physiological measures) might have altered their results? Why or why not?

Chapter 3

1. In his article, Brendan Keogh contends that the study by Whitaker and Bushman does not connect violent video games with real-life gun violence. What are his reasons? Do you agree or disagree?

2. Explain what Jesse Aaron means when he says that the main reasons for cyberbullying are the false ideations of "someone deserving it." Do you agree or disagree? Why or why not?

3. Patrick Stafford's article relates some game developers' beliefs that the cold, emotionless heroes in video games serve as poor role models that can translate into children becoming less emotional and more likely to bully or harass others. What is Rosalind Wiseman's solution? Do you agree or disagree that a solution is needed? Is Wiseman's a valid solution?

Chapter 4

1. In the article by Joyram and Nirali Chakraborty, the authors point out that there is no cohesive policy regarding areas that may cause harm to minors. What are the differences in how governing agencies determine whether or not to take action? Should there be a cohesive policy in this area? If so, what should it be?

2. Discuss the Supreme Court's decision in the case of *Brown v. Entertainment Merchant's Association*. Do you support the reasons for the decision? Why or why not?

3. In her article, Alyssa Rosenberg states that she believes people have become overly concerned with "avoiding being violently killed." List her reasons for this opinion. Do you agree or disagree?

Organizations to Contact

The editors have compiled the following list of organizations concerned with the issues debated in this book. The descriptions are derived from materials provided by the organizations. All have publications or information available for interested readers. The list was compiled on the date of publication of the present volume; the information provided here may change. Be aware that many organizations take several weeks or longer to respond to inquiries, so allow as much time as possible.

The Center for Successful Parenting
website: http://www.centersuccessparenting.com

This non-profit organization was "established to help educate parents and grandparents about the pervasive negative effects that media violence has on America's children," for which they raise money to run a national awareness campaign.

Entertainment Consumer's Association (ECA)
email: info@theeca.com
website: http://www.theeca.com

This non-profit membership organization represents consumers of digital entertainment in the US and Canada. It was founded to give gamers a collective voice with which to communicate concerns, address issues and focus on advocacy efforts. It is committed to public policy efforts and empowering and enabling the membership to effect change. It has local chapters in a majority of states. To read its stance on violence and video games, check here: http://www.theeca.com/video_games_violence.

Entertainment Software Rating Board
website: http://www.esrb.org

Established in 1994 by the Entertainment Software Association (ESA), this non-profit organization assigns ratings to video games and apps in order to afford parents the ability to make informed choices when purchasing games and apps for their children. Rating categories include age-appropriateness, content, and interactive elements. The categories are age-based and offer concise and impartial content information.

Illinois Institute for Addiction Recovery
phone: 800-522-3784
website: http://www.addictionrecov.org/Addictions/?AID=45

Though this institute addresses all forms of addiction, it includes addiction to video games, which can happen when "impairments of real life relationships are disrupted as a result of excessive use of the Game." In-patient as well as daytime treatment plans are available.

The Megan Meier Foundation
515 Jefferson, Suite A., St. Charles, MO 63301
phone: 636-757-3501
email: info@meganmeierfoundation.org
website: http://www.meganmeierfoundation.org

Founded in 2007, the mission of this foundation is to support actions to end bullying, cyberbullying and suicide. Its vision is "to live in a world where bullying and cyberbullying no longer exist." They offer presentations, counseling services, and scholarship opportunities for kids who make a positive impact in their community in regard to the issues of bullying and cyberbullying. Their workshop, EMPOWER, is an interactive student bullying & cyberbullying prevention training program.

Mothers Against Videogame Addiction and Violence (MAVAV)
website: http://www.mavav.org

The Mothers Against Videogame Addiction and Violence is an organization, founded in 2002, whose goal is to educate parents on what they consider an addiction and an epidemic. Their methodology is to document the harmful effects of video games and their impact on current culture. They believe that video games are addictive, lead to youth violence, isolation, and desensitization, and are an inferior medium to films and literature. They offer news, articles, and current and archived forums.

Parents Television Council (PTC)
707 Wilshire Boulevard #2075, Los Angeles, CA 90017
phone:(213) 403-1300; (800) 882-6868 (Toll-Free)
website: http://w2.parentstv.org/Main/campaigns/vvideo.aspx

The Parents Television Council is a non-partisan organization that advocates for responsible entertainment. The mission of PTC is to protect children and families from graphic sex, violence and profanity in the media; their vision, to provide a safe entertainment media environment for children and families across America. They offer news articles, research, a blog, and a parent "toolkit" for TV viewing and information.

Stomp Out Bullying™
phone: (877) 602-8559
website: http://www.stompoutbullying.org/index.php
/about/mission

Established in 2005, Stomp Out Bullying™ is the leading bullying and cyberbullying prevention organization in America. Its focus is educating about all forms of violence in schools and online and teaching how to respond to all forms of bullying through various means, including peer mentoring and social media campaigns.

Bibliography of Books

C.A. Anderson, K.E. Buckley, and D.A. Gentile. *Violent video game effects on children and adolescents: Theory, research, and public policy.* New York, NY: Oxford Univ. Press, 2007.

Karen E. Dill. *How Fantasy Becomes Reality: Seeing through Media Influence.* New York, NY: Oxford University Press, 2009.

Joe Dilley. *The Game Is Playing Your Kid: How to Unplug and Reconnect in the Digital Age.* Minneapolis, MN: Bascom Hill, 2015.

R. Espejo. *Violent video games.* Farmington Hills, MI: Greenhaven Press, 2015.

Richard Freed. *Wired Child: Reclaiming Childhood in a Digital Age.* North Charleston, SC: CreateSpace Independent Publishing Platform, 2015.

Diane Marczely Gimpel. *Violence in Video Games.* Minneapolis, MN: Abdo, 2013.

D. Grossman and G. DeGaetano. *Stop teaching our kids to kill: A call to action against TV, movie & video game violence.* New York, NY: Crown, 1999.

Barrie Gunter. *Does Playing Video Games Make Players More Violent?* London, UK: Palgrave Macmillan, 2016.

Mary Heston. *Violent Games-Violent Children?* Las Vegas, NV: Internet Medical Association, 2011.

Gerard Jones. *Killing Monsters: Why Children Need Fantasy, Super Heroes, and Make-believe Violence.* New York, NY: Basic Books, 2002.

Nicholas Kardaras. *Glow Kids: How Screen Addiction Is Hijacking Our Kids—and How to Break the Trance.* New York, NY: St. Martin's Press, 2016.

Steven J Kirsh. *Children, Adolescents, and Media Violence: A Critical Look at the Research.* Thousand Oaks, CA: Sage Publications, 2006.

Kathy Koch. *Screens and Teens: Connecting with Our Kids in a Wireless World.* Chicago, IL: Moody Press, 2015.

Rachel Kowert and Thorsten Quandt. *The Video Game Debate: Unravelling the Physical, Social, and Psychological Effects of Digital Games.* New York, NY: Routledge, 2015.

L. Kutner. *Grand theft childhood: The surprising truth about violent video games and what parents can do.* New York, NY: Simon & Schuster, 2008.

P.M. Markey and Christopher J. Ferguson. *Moral combat: Why the war on violent video games is wrong.* Dallas, TX: Benbella Books, 2017.

A. Melzer and C. Happ. *Empathy and Violent Video Games: Aggression and Prosocial Behavior.* London, UK: Palgrave Macmillan, 2014.

Torill Elvira Mortensen, Jonas Linderoth and Ashley M.L. Brown. *The Dark Side of Game Play: Controversial Issues in Playful Environments.* New York, NY: Routledge, 2015.

Andrea C. Nakaya. *Thinking Critically: Video Games and Violence.* San Diego, CA: ReferencePoint Press, 2013.

Patricia D. Netzley. *How Does Video Game Violence Affect Society?* San Diego, CA: ReferencePoint Press, 2012.

Jaclyn Schildkraut and H. Jaymi Elsass. *Mass Shootings: Media, Myths, and Realities.* Santa Barbara, CA: Praeger, 2016.

Gareth Schott. *Violent Games: Rules, Realism, and Effect 3.* New York, NY: Bloomsbury Academic, 2016.

Kaveri Subrahmanyam and David Šmahel. *Digital Youth: The Role of Media in Development.* New York, NY: Springer, 2011.

Bonnie Szumski and Jill Karson. *How Does Violent Media Affect Youth?* San Diego, CA: ReferencePoint Press, 2014.

Greg Toppo. *The Game Believes in You: How Digital Play Can Make Our Kids Smarter.* New York, NY: St. Martin's Press, 2015.

Ryan G. Van Cleave. *Unplugged: My Journey into the Dark World of Video Game Addiction.* Deerfield Beach, FL: Health Communications, 2010.

Peter Vorderer and Jennings Bryant. *Playing Video Games: Motives, Responses, and Consequences.* Mahwah, NJ: Lawrence Erlbaum Associates, 2006.

Wayne Warburton and Danya Braunstein. *Growing up Fast and Furious: Reviewing the Impacts of Violent and Sexualised Media on Children.* Annandale, NSW: Federation Press, 2012.

Mark J. P. Wolf. *The Video Game Explosion: A History from PONG to Playstation and beyond.* Westport, CT: Greenwood Press, 2008.

Garry Young. *Ethics in the Virtual World: The Morality and Psychology of Gaming.* New York, NY: Routledge, 2014.

Index